Small Miracles

Coping with infertility, miscarriage, stillbirth
and premature birth

Rachel Stanfield-Porter

and

the Bonnie Babes Foundation

hachette
AUSTRALIA

⌂ hachette
AUSTRALIA

Published in Australia and New Zealand in 2009
by Hachette Australia
(An imprint of Hachette Australia Pty Limited)
Level 17, 207 Kent Street, Sydney NSW 2000
www.hachette.com.au

Copyright © Rachel Stanfield-Porter (and the Bonnie Babes Foundation) 2009

National Library of Australia
Cataloguing-in-Publication data

Stanfield-Porter, Rachel

Small Miracles: coping with infertility, miscarriage, stillbirth and premature birth / Rachel Stanfield-Porter, Bonnie Babes Foundation.

ISBN 978 0 7336 2446 9 (pbk.)

Pregnancy – Complications.
Miscarriage.
Infants – Death.
Fetal death.
Stillbirth.
Bereavement.
Grief.

Other authors/Contributors: Bonnie Babes Foundation.

155.937

Cover design by Caz Hoad of Triad Communications
Photograph of Aria on page 219 reproduced with permission of her mother, Veronica Lees.
Text design by Bookhouse, Sydney
Typeset in 13.5/16 pt Perpetua
Printed in Australia by Griffin Press, Adelaide

Hachette Australia's policy is to use papers that are natural, renewable and recyclable products and made from wood grown in sustainable forests. The logging and manufacturing processes are expected to conform to the environmental regulations of the country of origin.

'I Celebrate Your Life, My Baby'
Music by Judith Durham © 1998 Musicoast
Words by Judith Durham, Rachel Stanfield-Porter, Simon Barnett © 1998
Musicoast/Bonnie Babes Foundation
Published by Musicoast Pty Ltd, PO Box 555, South Yarra, Victoria 3141, Australia
International Copyright Secured. All rights reserved. Unauthorised reproduction is illegal. For more information on Judith go to www.judithdurham.com.

Special thanks to Michael Newman and his company, brandnewman, for donating to the Bonnie Babes Foundation numerous strategic, brand and creative concepts, as well as the intellectual property including 'Small Miracles' (from which the title of the book comes). We are proud Michael is a life member of the Bonnie Babes Foundation.

Thanks to the Four Seasons hotel for hosting our board meetings and their support with accommodation for volunteers.

To my baby

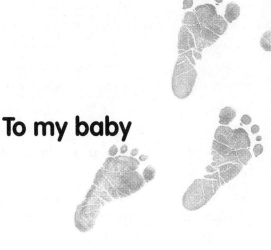

I wanted you so much. I was so excited when I discovered that you were on the way. We had been hoping to have a baby for a while and I really thought you were meant to be! The timing seemed so perfect; I never expected anything to go wrong.

I fell pregnant straightaway, I got all the symptoms; nausea, sore breasts and I felt so tired, I didn't mind though because you would have been worth it. I would have done anything to keep you.

I'll never understand why you didn't stay with me. You were all I thought about. I had such hopes and dreams for you; I just knew you were going to be beautiful. Ever since I was a little girl I'd wanted to be a mother. I'd waited a long time to have my dream fulfilled and now it would be... Well, I thought so then.

I feel so empty and alone since you left me and even though you were only part of my life for ten weeks, I'll never forget you. I never thought it possible to feel such a love and longing for someone. It hurts so much to know that I'll never hold you, never see you smile, never have you as part of my life. It doesn't seem right when I wanted you more than anything in the world.

I hope there's a heaven and that you're there. Maybe I'll get to meet you some day. In my heart and in my mind you'll always be my first child, the first fruits of your daddy's and my love.

I love you so much and I'm still very sad. I still think about you nearly every day and long to have you back again. I know I have let you go now, my baby; it's so hard to do. I want to be able to hope for a brother or sister, for one who will stay with me much longer than you were able to. I know you would have stayed if you could have. It wasn't your fault, it wasn't my fault, it wasn't your daddy's fault, you just couldn't stay and although I'll never know why, I'll try and accept that and keep on hoping for happier times in the future.

I will never forget you and I'll love you forever, from your Mummy.

'Some people walk in and out of our lives without making an impression . . . Others stay a while and take the time to leave footprints on our hearts . . . And we are never the same again.'

In the tenth week of pregnancy, a baby is generally 30 millimetres in length.

Contents

A note on sources & additional reading

Small Miracles aims to be an introduction to the emotional challenges of grief and recovery. It grew out of the need we have identified for individuals to share their very personal and human stories by way of coping with their grief and resolving their loss. The book's intention is to share with you those experiences rarely talked about in the hope that they are a validation of your feelings and a starting point for your emotional recovery and acceptance. All the interviews in this book were conducted by the Bonnie Babes Foundation, though not all families in the book have used the Bonnie Babes grief counselling services and some names have been changed. Additional information regarding suggested coping strategies and general medical information was provided by The Foundation's psychologists, counsellors and medical board. Although all statistics are correct at the time of printing, unfortunately some statistics in the medical field differ as information available can be lacking or conflicting. However, I know the importance of statistics, so have included the most consistent data for the most comprehensive overview with the assistance of the medical board. The statistic that one in four pregnancies ends in a loss takes into account those pregnancies that are lost before 20 weeks. These figures are an international statistic that has come out of the results of the most up-to-date research studies into miscarriage and pregnancy loss.

This book contains information obtained from authentic and highly regarded sources. Reasonable efforts have been made to publish reliable data and information, but the author and publisher cannot assume responsibility for the validity of all materials or for the consequences of their use.

The following publications were used in the research and preparation of this work: Bonnie Babes Foundation, *You are part of our lives and will always live in our hearts*; Bonnie Babes Foundation; *A Dad's Story*; Bonnie Babes Foundation; *Talking to children about grief and loss*; Borg, S. *When Pregnancy Fails*, Beacon Press, Boston, 1981; Deveson, Lord, J. *When a Baby Suddenly Dies*, Hill of Content, Melbourne, 1983; Friedman, R. *Surviving Pregnancy Loss*, Little Brown, Boston, 1982; Ilse, S, *Precious Lives, Painful Choices: a prenatal decision-making guide*, Wintergreen Press, 1993; Ilse, S. and Appelbaum, A. *Empty Arms: coping with miscarriage, stillbirth and infant death*, Wintergreen Press, 1982; McKissock, M. and McKissock, D., *Coping with Grief* (third edition), ABC Books, Sydney, 2008; Moffit, P. & Kohn, I. *Pregnancy Loss: A silent sorrow*, Routledge, US, 2000; Moulder, C. *Miscarriage: Women's experiences and needs*, Routledge, UK, 1992, 2001; Neugeboren, Jay, *An Orphan's Tale*, Holt, Rinehart and Winston, New York, c. 1976; Nicol, M. *Loss of a Baby: Understanding maternal grief*, Bantam Books, Sydney, 1989; Peppers, L. and Knapp, R. *Motherhood and Mourning*, Praeger, New York, 1980; Regan, L. *Miscarriage: what every woman needs to know, a positive new approach*, Bloomsbury Publishing, 1997; Rousselot, S. *Avoiding miscarriage: Everything you need to know to feel more confident in pregnancy*, Sea Change Press, US, 2006; Ryan, A. *A Silent Love: Personal stories of coming to terms with miscarriage*, Penguin Books, Ringwood, Victoria, 2000; Schiff, H. *The Bereaved Parent*, Penguin Books, New York, 1978.

How to use this book

There is always someone to talk to, there is always someone to help.

Not every pregnancy ends with the joy of holding your baby in your arms – this is the experience of many thousands of Australian women and their partners every year. Everyone's story is unique and no less important or valid than anyone else's. The sense of loss, grief and the many roads to emotional recovery are all very different. This book aims to offer a pragmatic and very human collection of voices offering validation, consolation and hope in the face of the very complex and diverse area of personal grief after the loss of a baby through infertility, miscarriage, stillbirth, neonatal loss and premature birth. It is not intended to be a comprehensive exploration of the topic and offers only introductory medical information. The book aims to offer, first and foremost, consolation and coping strategies to help the reader better interpret and understand their experiences and inspire them to begin their emotional recovery. Your grief journey is important, and we would encourage you to share your experience – to talk about it, to write about it, and above all to share your thoughts and your feelings with your friends and family.

The Bonnie Babes Foundation is the only organisation of its type in Australia and the charity is the leading organisation in the field of pregnancy loss, neonatal loss and issues relating to prematurely born babies. If you feel yourself or someone you know needs assistance, counselling or support when you read this book then call the Bonnie Babes Foundation on 1300 266 643 or go to the Foundation's website, www.bbf.org.au.

Foreword

I didn't know until it happened to me how devastating the loss of a baby can be. Not only to the parents, but their family: aunts, uncles, cousins, nephews, nieces and friends. All of the people who share the joy and anticipation that a new pregnancy brings to those who love and care for the expectant mum and dad.

Sadly it's a reality for as many as one in four pregnancies ends in miscarriage.

My first baby was born at 23 weeks and was unable to survive the first hour of his life. But I was lucky. Unlike many I had the wisdom of those around me who had been there before. The doctors, the nurses and the social workers at the Royal Hospital for Women, Randwick, encouraged me to look at my baby and to grieve the loss that was all so real.

We named him Isaac after my paternal grandfather, the hospital chaplain conducted the funeral and his ashes were scattered at my sister's farm where we planted a beautiful tree in his memory.

I was able to give my son a proper farewell and I take comfort in the knowledge that his tiny, lifeless body was treated with dignity and humanity.

But countless others are still coming to terms with their silent and often mysterious loss, a miscarriage or premature birth where the baby's body was expediently removed, and the overwhelming sadness as their emotions were swept under the carpet.

How many women, and men, still grieving their tragic loss, were inappropriately 'comforted' with the words, 'better luck next time'?

And whilst this advice was often well intended I know from my experience that it's important to embrace the reality and celebrate the child who might have been. For the months that I carried Isaac inside me we connected every moment of every day. I loved that little one so much and I took pleasure from the dreams and plans that I had for him and for us as a family.

Perhaps his greatest legacy is what he has left behind for his brother, our son Oscar now aged eight. Isaac taught me there is no greater gift than life and that you can't take anything for granted. Every day I cherish the fact that we were lucky to be given a second chance and deliver a healthy baby – life's most precious gift.

I hope that in some way my experience may help others to cope with their 'silent tears', the term often applied to those babies we have loved and lost. I truly believe it's important to share our stories and talk about the fact that approximately 70,000 babies don't make it every year. I congratulate Bonnie Babes on the extraordinary work they do to help those who have been to the edge and looked into the darkness. Their efforts not only help those suffering to deal with their grief but the Bonnie Babes Foundation also provides hope in a very real way by funding research and technologies that help premmie babies survive.

May this book be dedicated to all those babies who touched our lives for a moment but have changed our hearts forever.

Deborah Thomas
General Manager,
Editorial and Advertising Projects Women's Lifestyle,
ACP Magazines

Preface

Rachel's story – a silent tear

The realities of the scale of stillbirth and miscarriage is emphasised by Oprah, Courtney Cox-Arquette, Kerri-Anne Kennerley, Nicole Kidman and countless other famous people, sportspeople, and everyday people who experience the passing away of a baby, which for the most part is hidden from the outside world. Only in very recent times have these prominent people and celebrities come forward and spoken publicly about their losses.

Like silent tears wept over our precious babies, it's the silent loss sweeping the world and has been for generations. Extraordinarily the issue of stillbirth and miscarriage has been swept under the carpet, rarely talked about openly, women are told to 'try again', 'it's Nature's way', 'get on with life'.

It's time for that to change.

Should I try again for a new mother if my mother passes away? Is it nature's way if Dad dies of cancer? Should I get on with life if my sister dies in a car accident? The death of a baby is also a significant event in life and families deserve dignity and support.

What drives me is a memory, etched forever, of the silent tear on the face of a young blue-eyed, dark-haired mother in the bed next to mine, who sat propped up by pillows, breastfeeding her newborn son, the day my own son passed away.

As our eyes met, my own silent tears ran down my face as the realisation of the tragedy I had just experienced overwhelmed my senses and pounded through my body.

I'd been placed in a maternity ward. I could hear the echo of the newborn babies all around me crying in the nursery. The hospital baby crib, with my son Joshua's name on it, sat empty.

One mother, cradling her newborn, cried for another mother's empty arms.

Those silent tears and the desperately devastating sense of loss of my babies profoundly changed my life forever.

At the foot of my bed was a sign that read, 'Spontaneous abortion' in bold red letters. As I staggered from the bed to go to the ladies, I was stunned to see the sign – I squinted through my swollen, tear-filled eyes, and realised why I had been on the receiving end of cold stares from the other patients and visitors. They thought I had, by choice, aborted my son. This attitude also reflected an antiquated hospital system at the time, but things are much improved these days.

Two years earlier, I had been sent home from the emergency section in a major maternity hospital in Melbourne. After a rushed examination, following a 2½-hour wait, I was told I had superficial bleeding and was advised to, 'Calm down.'

It was a day that changed my life.

While I sat anxiously in the hectic emergency area, the nurse evaluating the patients and their priority commented to another nurse about a woman, 'Only a few months, just a bit of bleeding . . . she can wait,' then, as she motioned towards me, 'She is pregnant and may lose it.' Again, modern-day medical staff in these situations are trained and counselled to respond with sensitivity and an awareness of how a patient is feeling, particularly an anxious mother-to-be. Medical staff step forward and they join our grief counselling training courses with incredible dedication and commitment to help.

However, at the time of my loss, I was hardly being treated as a person and the little person inside me even less so. I was told to go home and phone the hospital if I had further concerns. Within hours, baby Ezra was expelled at home while I was alone. That sounds cold and clinical, it wasn't like that, it was awful and immediate and devastating, but I don't know the single right word, or how to explain easily how I felt. My life has been about controlled emotion and this is the first time I have 'talked' about it publicly in such detail.

We buried Ezra's remains in the backyard, marking his place with a cross. No one really spoke about it in our family. I still don't know if they really understood how we felt. Neighbours and distant friends who were not told straightaway continued to ask when the baby was due.

I closed the door on the nursery and packed away the baby clothes. I threw myself back into my hectic career. I was always good at bouncing back . . . or so I thought.

This was one of the reasons I founded the Bonnie Babes Foundation over 15 years ago. I've since met hundreds of families after the loss of their own babies. I've also travelled to other countries, establishing branches of the charity in the United States, New Zealand and the United Kingdom, and I have spoken to a considerable number of health professionals.

I realised my personal experience was being repeated in thousands of tragic ways, every day, every year and something had to be done, someone needed to come forward.

At times Bonnie Babes has been so difficult, the exhaustion of late nights, early mornings, weekends, the lack of resources, the lack of public understanding. Funds that were never provided by the government, sponsorships you held your breath for and hoped would materialise. We saw many other causes receive enormous recognition while the issues of infertility, miscarriage, stillbirth and premature babies were never adequately acknowledged. While the team at Bonnie Babes were happy that well deserving charities were acknowledged, they also felt Bonnie Babes deserved awareness and the funds to continue its worthy work. The charity deserved to rise above the struggle after almost 15 years.

It's been a rocky, painful, emotionally draining ride, but it's also been more fulfilling than I could have ever imagined. It's been a privilege I never expected and it's been the realisation that, if you have enough passion, you can truly make it happen and the most painful times in your life can be turned into something positive to help others.

It was immediately after the birth of Daniel, my third son, as the midwife handed me this incredibly precious child, that I turned to my husband Allan and said, 'We are so lucky, some people might never experience this type of joy and fulfillment – we need to help those in our situation who need strength and hope to go on.'

Seventeen months later we were truly blessed again when Joel Beau-Allan Ezra arrived, 3.6 kilograms and very healthy.

We knew we needed to establish grief counselling and we needed to raise money for much-needed medical research in Australia. We never found out why our sons died too soon, but we knew by helping to fund the right medical research projects we could help others find answers.

I didn't realise at that time my vision would become the Bonnie Babes Foundation. We didn't know it would be our life's work and affect every aspect of our world. This is a global issue that needs to be recognised and validated around the world. The silent tears are for all the babies who were not privileged enough to be able to experience a full and productive life.

What started as a dream has become a passion, which is now shared with over 1,000 active volunteers across Australia and several hundred abroad.

The charity has now trained 2,843 counsellors and helps over 17,000 grieving families each year. We have some of the most eminent professors and doctors in Australia on our medical board. We print 20,000 grief books per year and 5000 each of 'A Dad's Story' and a children's grief book. All Bonnie Babes services are free, limited only by funds.

As Bonnie Babes grows and becomes busier, with more and more families desperately seeking support, I have not had a moment to look back until I started writing *Small Miracles*. Now I look back with pride on what Bonnie Babes has achieved, which has only been possible with the passion and dedication of so many volunteers across Australia. Each volunteer has helped to make a difference. I live in the present for the two beautiful children I am so lucky to have and I look forward to the future with hope.

I recognise how fortunate I have been to have a generous team of volunteers around me who continue to support the Foundation and myself. They are all ultimately responsible for the continued success of the charity.

When I started the journey around Australia interviewing families for this book, even with my years of experience in the area I still felt overwhelmed by candid stories and the raw honest emotions of loss, grief, pain and hope.

It was a travelling rollercoaster ride filled with boxes of tissues, followed by hugs and even smiles, sometimes laughter at the antics of premature babies who'd struggled to live but were now strong; healthy tearaway terrors, providing their parents with hilarious tales to repeat to others with love and joy. It was uplifting to hear how healthy and normal these kids are despite their rough journey into the world. Never far from my mind was the sad statistic of approximately 192 babies dying every day in Australia from stillbirth and miscarriage and one in ten babies being born prematurely.

When you read *Small Miracles,* you'll share these very human stories of pain, grief, sacrifice, hope, joy and many other expressions of vast emotion. Hopefully *Small Miracles* will help you gain a little insight into the inner thoughts and feelings of countless families who have been affected by loss over the years. *Small Miracles* is an ongoing story of our universal tragedy, tears and triumph over adversity.

You don't have to have experienced a loss to read this book. You may just want to help others and have a greater understanding. *Small Miracles* can provide that understanding as it is also a collection of stories of courage and inspiration to never give up hope.

Thank you for reading this book and being a part of our 'Small Miracles' journey.

Rachel Stanfield-Porter
Founder
Bonnie Babes Foundation Inc.

Chapter 1

I wanted you so much

We have a word, orphan, to describe someone who has lost their parents; but there's no word for parents who have lost their child.* There is only grief. It is an unnamed, unspoken tragedy that touches all families in some way. The fact is that one in every four Australian pregnancies ends in a loss. The human reality of this shocking statistic is that in 2007 over 70,000 babies died. Even more perplexing is the fact that figure of one in every four pregnancies ending in a loss hasn't changed in Australia for the last 60 years.

Advances in medical technology to significantly reduce this figure are as much a priority as the need to address our collective emotional response to the loss of a baby. 'It' is still not talked about much, or enough, even among friends and family. The loss of a baby through miscarriage, stillbirth and prematurity is a subject so often brushed aside in that reserved, stoic way that we have. Each person reacts differently. Men try to get on with things like work, and women hold their feelings deep and close. Sometimes it's the other way around. Friends don't know what to say, or how to react.

* Neugeboren, Jay, *An Orphan's Tale*

The line between immense heartbreak and the greatest possible joy is so thin. What do you say and how do you, and your family, remember, cope and recover – and find the courage to try again for another baby or accept it is not to be? *Small Miracles* is a collection of untold stories of these parents and the little Aussie babies who do survive traumatic pregnancies and prematurity – they are the real small miracles – that provide the most wonderful tales of love and purpose imaginable.

Losing a baby – the rhythm of life and loss

A precious pregnancy began and your hopes and dreams for a future with a child were going to be realised with this child. With the loss of your baby, your hopes and dreams for this time have been shattered as you face such an unfair tragedy. Whether you were pregnant for a short time, or a number of months, whether you delivered a stillborn baby or your new infant died shortly after birth, you will have come to know this special little person in your life. Take the time to think about what your baby meant to you and how you are feeling now.

You soon will be faced with many decisions. Do not take your decisions lightly and do not allow people to force you to make your decisions too quickly, no matter how well-meaning the advice is. It is time to say hello and goodbye to your baby, and only you and your partner will know what that special greeting and farewell will be. Look, listen and draw on the experiences of others to help you make your decisions, but always keep in mind that you will handle your loss differently, you will grieve differently and you will create special memories of your baby differently. You may experience intense grief that will wax and wane, come and go, but it is critical that your baby and the rhythm of life and loss is integrated into your life, the way you want it to happen. Make your decisions and trust and believe that you can make them for yourself and your baby.

When an unborn or newborn baby dies

Pregnancy loss is unfortunately a common experience for many couples. Families are often left feeling shocked and numb as they deal with their grief. Most parents grieve for the loss of their baby regardless of the gestation of the pregnancy and this grief can be expressed in a number of ways.

In today's society, parenthood is usually a planned event with expectations for a good outcome. It is a shock to parents when things do go wrong and that despite the huge advances in medical technology, babies are stillborn or miscarried. Pregnancy loss represents a devastating loss of unfulfilled dreams for the future, which begin before conception.

Parents, and particularly mothers, often blame themselves for the failure to produce a healthy baby. Many repeatedly go over in their minds the events of the previous weeks, trying to determine a possible cause. Some of the more common fears expressed by mothers are:

- Maybe if I had more rest.
- Maybe I should have eaten better.
- Was it because I was stressed?
- We shouldn't have had sexual intercourse, a drink, etc . . .

In fact, it is unlikely that anything the parents did or did not do was the cause of the problem, as the actual cause is often not confirmed.

The physical experience of pregnancy loss can vary considerably. Some women experience pain and bleeding, while others are diagnosed on an ultrasound without any warning symptoms. If the pregnancy is lost in the early stages (a miscarriage), the mother may require no treatment or a curette to remove pieces of the pregnancy tissue from the uterus, which if left, can cause heavy bleeding and infection. If the pregnancy is further developed, the mother must labour to deliver the baby (stillbirth). It is a traumatic experience to labour for hours and not have a live baby at the end.

Depending on the stage at which the pregnancy is lost, it may be possible to see and hold the baby. Many parents are afraid of this at first, but in the majority of cases they have commented that it was a special time for them. Another way to remember the baby and help create an individual identity is to give the baby a name. Many hospitals have 'memory folders' in which photographs and other mementoes can be placed for keepsake.

Babies born after 20 weeks of pregnancy receive a birth and death certificate and cremation and burial arrangements can be made. Burial or cremation for babies born before 20 weeks is also possible to arrange but is not a legal requirement. Some hospitals offer a burial service but parents may prefer to arrange a private service to suit their needs. There is no right or wrong decision and it will depend on the individual feelings and beliefs.

Parents can feel the pregnancy loss is not recognised or acknowledged by those around them. Friends and family may seem to avoid mentioning the baby for fear of upsetting the parents or may not understand the extent of their grief. It is often helpful in these circumstances to refer to the baby by name – acknowledging the baby as part of the family. Talking with other parents who have had similar experiences can also be helpful. Often it is a surprise to find out that many other couples have experienced a loss and have felt similar feelings and grief.

Dealing with your fear, emotions and distress

You do not have to be strong or feel guilty about your loss, and it is okay to cry, scream and yell to express what you feel. Many emotions will come and go as time goes on and as you and your partner come to terms with your loss. In the weeks following your loss you will grieve for what might have been. The empty cot, the drawers filled with small clothes, the nursery, are all reminders that your baby won't be coming home. Your grief may overwhelm you and at other times the situation might not seem quite real.

There are no right or wrong ways of feeling or dealing with the grief of losing a baby and everyone copes in their own way. Over time your grief will change and move from the initial intensity on hearing the news. However, the effect of losing a baby will never leave you and you will never forget your baby.

Getting support and counselling

Grieving for your baby is difficult as you will be mourning the loss of a little being that you never got to know properly. Remember that you are not alone in your grief and that getting support from either close friends or family or counselling services can help you make sense of the emotions and the pain that you will be feeling. Don't be afraid of asking for help or a sympathetic listener. Being able to verbalise and express your feelings openly will help with the way in which you grieve. If you are looking for counselling, it is important that you feel comfortable and reassured talking to someone outside your circle of family and friends.

Learning to cope with the death of a baby

Don't rush your grief, make your own time
Give yourself time to feel your grief. The time it takes for you to experience the different stages of grief and a range of emotions will depend on you and no one else. Other people may offer well-meaning advice to help you, but you must follow your instincts and your own sense of timing to get to a point of feeling that you can comfortably deal with your grief.

Understand the grieving process
Grief often happens in stages moving between denial, anger, guilt, depression and acceptance. Understanding that there are many facets when experiencing grief will help you make sense of what feels like a rollercoaster ride of emotions.

You may have setbacks but this is a natural part of grief and remembering your baby
You might stall along the road to acceptance and you might find that some of your initial intense feelings of grief will

creep back, particularly on anniversaries or events that may trigger memories of your baby. Accept these setbacks and that they are difficult to face. It is okay to feel this way. If necessary, remove yourself from any situation that might trigger any feelings that you are not ready for until you feel strong enough to handle any potentially painful situations.

Talk with your partner

At this time it is normal for both you and your partner to retreat and deal with grief in your own way. Try to use this time to talk openly about how you are both feeling. Don't expect your partner to feel the same way as you do but allow yourself to be honest with your partner about how you feel.

Common Questions

I feel so guilty. Is this normal?

Guilt is one of the most common and intense feelings that parents deal with after the loss of their baby. It is a normal part of the grieving process. As a parent, it is understandable to wonder if there was something that could have been done to prevent this from happening. Always discuss this feeling of guilt with your partner and try not to move towards blaming one another. Don't be hard on yourself by going over and over what could have been done differently, how things could be different or raising the question, 'What if?' Try to keep your guilt under control by acknowledging that, whatever the circumstances, you and your partner did the best that you could do and events were beyond your control.

Why me? It isn't fair!

There is no rational reason. Your loss is terrible and it isn't fair. You might wonder why this is happening and what you did to cause this or maybe you feel that you deserved this loss. It is important to accept that the loss of your baby has happened, that you don't deserve it and that there is probably not a clear-cut reason as to why it happened.

What do I do now?

The pain of losing your baby is difficult and intense but you need to keep moving through it and the intensity of feelings will lessen with time. The memory of your baby will still be painful but you will come to terms or learn to accept your loss in your own way and in your own time.

Resources

Bonnie Babes Foundation – Head Office
PO Box 407
Canterbury, Vic, 3126
Phone: (03) 9803 1800 or 1300 266 643
Email: enquiry@bbf.org.au
Bonnie Babes Foundation – QLD
President – Barbara Short
PO Box 5843
Stafford Heights, QLD, 4053
Phone: (07) 3353 6285
Email: bbfqld@optusnet.com.au
(branches in every state of Australia)
www.bbf.org.au

The Bonnie Babes Foundation is the leading organisation in Australia in the field of pregnancy loss.

Post and AnteNatal Depression Association (PaNDa) is a Victorian-based self-help group for women who experience postnatal depression or postnatal psychosis.
810 Nicholson Street, North Fitzroy, VIC, 3068
Phone: (03) 9481 3377 or 1300 726 306
Email: info@panda.org.au
www.panda.org.au

Chapter 2

Understanding grief, guilt and loss

For many parents, the instant you knew you were pregnant, your life changed forever. Whether you were feeling joy or apprehension, this new baby was an important part of your future. The feelings you have after the death of a baby can be overwhelming and intense. You will not only begin a journey of recovering physically, but also emotionally and spiritually. Grief is the natural response to any loss. Parents need to be reminded how important it is to acknowledge all feelings, thoughts and emotions that will come up in the different stages of the grieving process.

Grieving after losing a baby

It is frequently said that the grief of bereaved parents is the most intense grief known. When a child dies, parents feel that a part of them has died, that a vital and core part of them has been taken away. 'It is impossible to understand how much a parent loves a child until that child is gone.' Grieving parents have to deal with the contradiction of wanting to be free of the overwhelming pain of the loss, yet wanting to remember the pain in order to have a reminder of the child who died. Grieving parents will always feel the empty place in their hearts caused by a child's death.

Parental grief can and often does involve a vast range of conflicting emotions and responses including shock and numbness, intense sadness and pain, depression, and often feelings of total confusion and disorganisation. Sometimes parents may not even seem sure of who they are and may feel as if they have lost an integral part of their very being. Grieving parents need to know how important it is to express their pain to someone who will understand and acknowledge what they are feeling and saying. They should be honest with themselves and others about how they feel. They should allow themselves to cry, be angry and complain. It is okay to admit to themselves that they are feeling overwhelmed, distracted and unable to focus or concentrate.

As with their approach to life, men and women may respond differently due to different gender needs and emotions. In death, men and women may also grieve differently. The mother may be deeply grieving, in a phase of searching and yearning, while the father has moved beyond this stage to an acceptance and resolution phase. The mother may view the father as cold and uncaring, an individual with whom she cannot share her feelings, which increases her sense of isolation and fails to allow her to recognise her grief. The father, on the other hand, in reaction to his discomfort at seeing his partner's distress, may see her as being over-emotional. This can often place stress on the parents' relationship at this very difficult time. It is important that parents keep talking to each other about the way they are feeling.

A mother's grief

Carrying a baby to term involves a complex interaction between baby and mother. For many women, the most difficult aspect of stillbirth or miscarriage is the emotional aftermath. The physical pain, and sometimes this is extreme pain, is short term. The emotional effects may continue for years. When a baby who is still a physical part of a woman's body dies, the mother may feel that a part of her dies too.

With the loss of a baby the mother may experience a strong feeling of disappointment and a sense of failure. A woman can feel like she has failed her child and also failed in the most basic role of what it means to be a woman. This sense of failure usually results in feelings of guilt at having disappointed her partner by being unable to give birth to a healthy child – this feeling is also difficult to express to her partner and can heighten the associated feeling of guilt.

Women can also feel that they have done something wrong to have caused the pregnancy loss. Sometimes it is concern about what was eaten, what was lifted, what chemicals she came in contact with. It seems to be a natural part of the grief over the loss of a baby that the mother feels that she hasn't protected her baby properly. This feeling also adds to the feeling of guilt that the mother experiences after a loss.

Losing a baby places a mother on a journey that has a beginning, but with the death of a baby there is no middle and no end to the story. The hopes and dreams a mother had for her child are abruptly stopped, and a mother may feel as if she is unfinished – her identity as a mother changes to the outside world, even though she is still and always will be a mother.

A father's grief

Despite our society's attitude that the traditional role of the male is changing, men are still expected to be 'strong' and show little emotion after the loss of their child. For many, tears of joy and tears of grief in a man are not entirely comfortable or acceptable. Along with this, the father is expected to protect his mate from the harsh realities of the world. This protective role may become untenable for the father. Particularly with fathers of stillborn children, they often feel that they could not protect the child during the pregnancy and have not had the opportunity to nurture that child.

When a baby dies, the anguish of the mother is visible to the world because she has the physical experience of pregnancy and giving birth. This does not happen for fathers. They can feel overlooked and feel that the concern for their loss is not as great as the mother's. Fathers also seem to cope differently, ranging from worry, ignoring the problem, focusing on work, turning from friends and keeping to themselves. Basically fathers have a tendency to deal with grief internally and to outward appearances they 'put on a brave face'.

As a man allows himself to feel the emotions associated with the loss of his child, he may also experience a sense of isolation, feeling that there is no one with whom he can share his grief. He may experience some inner conflict about sharing his grief with his partner for fear of upsetting her, increasing her feelings of grief or depressing her further.

There are also outside pressures on fathers who are expected to 'hold things together' and go back to work and to function as if nothing has happened. Time off from work for extended periods is sometimes not an acceptable situation for men and they have to deal with insensitive attitudes in the workplace.

Feelings of anger and hurt

Anger and hurt can ebb and flow during the grieving process. At times of grief, when help is desperately needed to deal with the emotional pain, many people do close off from friends and family as they try to deal with their personal turmoil. Anger and hurt manifest in many ways, such as laying blame on those closest – husbands, partners, medical professionals. It is also not unusual for feelings of jealousy and resentment to surface, particularly when other people are seen to be enjoying healthy pregnancies or on seeing families with healthy children.

A father can experience anger and frustration when his attempts to comfort and lessen his partner's emotional distress appear to fail or be ineffective. There can also be anger felt at what is seen to be insensitivity of people not fully understanding the loss of their child and the depth of the grief that is being felt.

Telling family and friends

Many couples can struggle with how best to let people in their lives know about a recent pregnancy loss. Breaking this news might also feel difficult if family and friends have been supportive of and excited about the pregnancy.

Keep it simple – you don't have to give a lot of information about what has happened. Share whatever information you are comfortable sharing with others. Don't be afraid to use the phone, to write or email if you need to let a wide circle of friends and family know. Tell your immediate family and close group of friends in person and use email or similar for general contact.

If you are finding it really difficult to tell people, and if people are waiting to hear the news of your new baby, see if a close friend or relative might be willing to contact people for you. This can take the pressure off you and your partner giving you time to deal with the news of the loss in your own time.

Surviving insensitivity

Many people don't understand the power, depth, intensity, or duration of grief that parents deal with after a loss of their baby. In some instances, the parents may be ignored because some people are not able to deal with the tragedy and do not know what to say for fear of upsetting the parents further. Many people simply don't know what to say and so won't do anything. People often cannot understand the loss because it was not a baby who they saw or held. This can mean it is sometimes hard for others to know how to help.

People do try to help. They do not know what to say or they say what they feel is right. Society prepares us for death and old age to come together. We are not prepared for birth and death to be so close together. When an adult dies there are words to say but when a child lost is from a miscarriage or stillbirth or was a newborn baby, people often become distant or feel awkward.

Sometimes people will say things that are unintentionally hurtful or seem insensitive, particularly if they have not experienced pregnancy loss and have no idea what to say to comfort the parents. Things that might be said include, 'At least you can get pregnant', 'You can always try again', 'Everything will be fine next time', 'It was meant to be', 'It happened because—'.

As difficult as it is at the time to hear these types of comments, you can always speak out and let people know how you are feeling if you feel the comment is not appropriate. You can always respond as calmly as possible by telling the person how you feel about the particular comment, changing the subject or trying to gently educate the person about your circumstances. Keep in mind that people are genuinely trying to deal with your grief in their own way.

Kirstie's story

Kirstie Marshall is Australia's first world champion skier, winning 17 World Cup gold medals. She was named Australian Skier of the Year six times and Victorian Sportswoman of the Year four times. Kirstie was elected as the Member for Forest Hill in the State Parliament of Victoria in 2002, and re-elected in 2006.

Through my skiing career, I have faced many pressure-filled situations and come through them relatively unscathed, but I wasn't sure whether this would transfer to what I think is the most challenging situation of all — having children.

Originally I was pregnant with twins and then on the second scan, only one was viable. To this day, I am grateful I didn't lose both.

Kirstie's story shows how the grief of losing a baby can remain with you forever.

In conversation with a family friend I made an off-the-cuff comment upon noticing some weeds, 'Isn't it unbelievable that these weeds can grow here?' I was shocked when the response was, 'That's what I said . . . After my Elisabeth died, I said to my own mum, how is it that God can let a weed grow but can take my Elisabeth?'

Kirstie remembers being so surprised that her friend, who is over 80 years old, still remembers the intense feeling of the grief for her own lost child.

I still feel emotional when I think that someone could go through life and weeds remind them of their lost child . . . I still feel so sad for her.

Kirstie's sense of personal loss is a reflection of what other mothers who have lost their child may feel. In some cases women have been sent death certificates even if no birth certificate was issued, while others never receive a birth certificate as the baby had not been born. This highlights the need for some sensitivity from the various public and medical bodies when approaching the loss of babies preterm.

I think that these issues for women are thought of as 'women's problems' as opposed to 'people's problems'. When that perception changes, dealing with these early deaths for many people will be a lot better and a lot easier. That is something we can all aim for.

small miracles

Adrienne's story

Adrienne Ryan is a former councillor and Mayor of
Ku-ring-gai Council in Sydney, New South Wales. She
is also the author of *A Silent Love*, a book that details
her experience of dealing with the loss of multiple
miscarriages.

*The reason I wrote the book was because when I started to lose
those babies [Adrienne lost six babies], I was looking for things to
read and to know that other people had been through a similar
situation . . .*

*I wanted somebody else to have suffered in the same way. It
was almost a nasty feeling; I felt very guilty feeling [this way],
and I needed to know that other people felt the same.*

Adrienne couldn't find much information on how to
deal with the grief of the loss of her babies, and as she
suffered more and more losses, she decided that she would
put her experience to good use and compile a book of her
experiences and other women's experiences, to help other
parents feel less isolated and alone in their silent grief.

*. . . the greatest gift that you can give [yourself] is to acknowl-
edge that you had a child and it isn't a child that can be replaced,
it isn't just a loss . . . it's a loss of a member of the family.*

The father's grief should also be acknowledged, even
though men grieve in very different ways.

*It's the father's loss as well. When flowers came to me and it
was just to 'Adrienne', and not 'Peter and Adrienne', it hurt my
husband that people didn't recognise that it was his loss as well.
Men feel that they have to be strong. They have to be strong for
you because the wife is so devastated and you don't necessarily
give the men permission to grieve.*

Another valuable message is the acknowledgement from others of a couple having a child and losing it. Adrienne realises that people don't want to acknowledge the loss because it is too hard for them to deal with or find the right words to say to comfort the parents.

Barry's story

Barry is a director of photography who owns his own company and has been involved in the TV industry for many years.

Barry gives an insight into how he felt as a father, dealing with the loss of his baby, Madison. His candid story shows how men and women may grieve very differently and, at times, the emotional stress and strain can often prove too much for some relationships.

My wife was 37. We'd decided to go to one of Melbourne's major maternity hospitals and have a natural birth. The public health system copes incredibly well, but at the point that Carol went into labour we were many weeks over average term. That should have sounded some warning bells, but didn't. Carol and I persisted with a natural birth. A strained public health system comes apart when things just go a little off; heart monitoring failed, there was a bit of a scurry to get another machine and a bit of time taken for the decision that we really should be off to Emergency. The surgeon performed a caesarean, but Carol's heart wasn't strong enough. I coped in the only way that I knew — I went and shot a commercial, tried to get on with my life.

The counsellor at the hospital was really difficult because I just wanted to get on with things, but they were adamant that I should address matters.

Just organising the funeral was hideous. I went to the funeral and the woman made such an issue of it. We just wanted a celebration and we wanted Madison's ashes put in a family rose garden. It was simple in our mind . . . if it was a feature film, you would cut the scene because it was over-dramatic, it was just nuts.

After the stillbirth of their first child, Barry and Carol had trouble conceiving, which also put a strain on the relationship, particularly with Barry dealing with his grief by trying to return to a life before their first baby.

We went to great lengths [to conceive again] but Carol had a lot of trouble conceiving. Who knows whether it was my behaviour, whether it was my work and drinking, or whether it was her tension and remorse, but finally we took some time off and went for a holiday and, bang, she was pregnant, and we had Nellie.

I should have been there for her, I guess I just didn't know what to say or do. I still don't.

Carol's story

Carol is Barry's ex-wife. Listening to Barry's story was the first time she had heard him verbalise the pain he went through many years ago.

Carol clearly outlines what it feels like to be a mother, carrying a child and connecting with the baby during pregnancy.

Barry and I got together in 1989 and, as Barry said, he was working, very hard, focusing on his business. The baby was always very active during the pregnancy. I was nurturing this child, talking to her and having a relationship with her. Because she was so active I was always aware of her, so from my perspective I was already a mother. But that differed a lot from Barry . . . I think he was waiting for her to arrive to then start a relationship with her.

After Madison's death, Carol explains how her way of dealing with grief was very emotional whereas she felt her kept his emotions under wraps and didn't openly talk about how he was feeling. Carol also found that it was difficult for other people to deal with Madison's death and, at times, she was met with some insensitivity to her situation that affected her deeply. With Barry seemingly in shutdown mode, Carol sought help with counsellors and tried to keep the memory of Madison alive.

Barry just couldn't talk about it, wouldn't deal with it.

It was hard to know what Barry was thinking or feeling because he was in work mode, and I was in grief mode. I couldn't stop crying, couldn't get over it, it was just devastating. I went to several counsellors. After I confronted unresolved grief from the death of my father when I was a child, I then became pregnant a couple of years later. Things hadn't changed much – Barry was still very quiet and didn't want to talk about it. I think there was a lot of 'holding back'.

Nellie's birth was clouded by Madison's death, and so was the relationship.

Our relationship did break down after Nellie was born. I was relieved in a way [several years after that], I needed to get away. The first thing I did after Barry left was to organise a funeral for Madison, because I really didn't want Madison's ashes in a box in the spare bedroom for the rest of my life.

I organised a memorial tree to be planted, a magnificent Bunya Bunya Pine, so that through all trees I could celebrate her life, every day, just by looking at any tree. We had a funeral service, scattered Madison's ashes on and around her tree, and with a few friends sang a couple of songs including 'Twinkle, Twinkle Little Star'.

I didn't invite my mum or my sister which later brought on anger because they were not included, and disappointment that there was no gravestone that they could visit. The belated funeral [three years later] was carried out purely for myself and Nellie and Madison. I was unaware of the loss felt by those around me.

On Madison's birthday we share a cake for her. My mum and my sister always send flowers to honour and acknowledge her memory, and I always shed tears and spend the day celebrating her birthday.

I now know that being the mother of Madison took me on a journey through some aspects of love . . . the strength of mother love . . . the pain of loss . . . and the courage to mother again.

Learning to cope with grief and the feeling of loss

The single most important factor in healing from the loss of your baby is having the support of other people. Even if you aren't comfortable talking about your feelings under normal circumstances, it may be important to express them when you're grieving. Sharing your loss makes the burden of grief easier to carry. Don't grieve alone; connecting with others will help you heal.

Finding support

- Family and friends – now is the time to lean on people who are close to you and let them know how you are feeling. Rather than avoiding people, which is easy to do when you are experiencing grief, accept any help whenever it is offered. Let family and friends know what you need as sometimes people don't know how to help out in a difficult situation.

- Talk to a therapist or counsellor if you feel that you aren't coping with your grief or are having trouble communicating with your partner. An experienced therapist can help you work through intense emotions and help you through the grief process.
- Join a support group if you are feeling lonely and isolated, if you need more support outside your circle of family and friends. Sharing with people who have similar experiences can help.

Look after yourself
- Grief impacts on the body and can cause symptoms such as sleeplessness, anxiety, a change in eating habits and gastrointestinal upsets. Take care of yourself by looking after your physical health and paying attention to your diet.
- Relaxation and sleep are really important to help bolster your emotional health. Schedule time every day to take time out for yourself with meditation, a walk, playing sport, having a bath, listening to music – anything that helps you relax. Try to get adequate sleep.
- Be realistic by being kind to yourself and accept that you need to grieve in the way that feels natural to you. Your grief is your own, and no one else can tell you when it is time to 'move on' or 'get over it'. Don't judge yourself against other people's ideas and beliefs.

Face your feelings
- Acknowledge your grief and how you are feeling. If you try to suppress the grief and keep up a strong face to the outside world, you can prolong the grief, which can lead to complications such as depression, anxiety, substance abuse, and long-term health problems.

Coping strategies
You may need to experiment to find out which strategies are most helpful for you. You could try:
- Crying – If you feel the need to cry, go ahead and do it. If there are no tears, this doesn't mean you are not grieving.
- Time alone – Make sure you allow yourself time alone every day to focus on your feelings and express them in whatever way fits with your ideas, such as writing in a journal or diary, remembering, memorials.
- Physical activity – This can often help release some tension associated with grief and give you a chance to be occupied with an activity that gives you a break from the intensity of your grief.
- Memorial – You might like to write letters to your baby, plant a tree, and put together an album of photographs. Buy a star from the International Star Registry (www.starregistry.com) and name it after your baby. Then you can see the star in the sky each night.
- Support team – Seek support through friends and family, your doctor, work colleagues, community health groups, online chat rooms, professional counsellors.
- Professional help – If you feel out of control or your emotions are becoming difficult to handle, seek the help of your doctor or health professional.

Common Questions

How long will this go on?

The journey through grief is a highly individual experience. Initially grief may be overwhelming and people can feel out of control. With time people find that they are able to choose when they can take time to remember or feel emotion for their loss. The intensity of grief is related to the degree of attachment to the person, relationship to the deceased, level of understanding and social support from others.

Am I going mad?

If a person feels that their grief is not in sync with social and cultural expectations, and/or have very intense grief, this can make them feel like they are out of control. Grief affects people physically, emotionally, psychologically and spiritually. Receiving validation and permission to grieve is an important part of the healing process.

Should I be feeling like this? Is it normal for my emotions to shift?

Grief includes a wide range of emotions, thoughts and behaviours. You may experience some or all of the following reactions. Your responses might even be contradictory at times.

- Anger
- Anxiety
- Change in worldview
- Confusion
- Sadness and depression
- Drop in self-esteem
- Difficulties in concentration

- Feeling unable to cope
- Guilt and remorse
- Helplessness
- Hopelessness
- Loneliness
- Questioning values and beliefs
- Relief
- Shock and disbelief

Is there a right way or a wrong way of coping with grief?

Everyone has a different way of coping and dealing with their grief, and this is also affected by life experiences. If a person receives support then the impact of grief will diminish and recovery can begin. Most important for the person grieving is talking about what is happening, what they are going through, how they are feeling, whether they are feeling comfortable expressing their emotions and feeling supported and accepted. Grief isn't predictable and everyone moves through grief in his or her own way.

Nobody seems to understand that I'm still grieving, what can I do?

It is difficult for someone who has never lost a baby to comprehend what you are going through. The best way to deal with others when you are grieving is to be honest and tell people what you need. Even if others are having a difficult time understanding your loss, allow yourself time to remember and honour your precious baby.

Do I need help?

Continuing fears or anxieties about your wellbeing or health or thoughts of self-harm should be addressed by seeking professional help. Extensive periods of intense emotion or obsessional thoughts or behaviour that makes day-to-day living difficult may also need outside help.

How do I move on?

There is an expectation that accepting the loss of a loved one means letting go of them and their memory. The reality is that many bereaved people continue to have a relationship with their loved one for the rest of their lives. Death ends a life, not a relationship.

Resources

Suggested reading:
Bonnie Babes Foundation, *A Dad's Story*
McKissock, M. and McKissock, D., *Coping with Grief* (third edition), ABC
Books, Sydney, 2008

Australian Centre for Grief and Bereavement
The Australian Centre for Grief and Bereavement is an independent,
not-for-profit organisation, which opened in January 1996.
Freecall (Australia wide): 1800 664 786
www.grief.org.au

Crisis Care
Crisis Care is a free telephone counselling information and referral
service that runs 24 hours a day and is staffed by trained counsellors
who will listen and offer help and support to anyone who needs it on
1800 199 008.

Lifeline Crisis Counselling
Lifeline has a 24-hour crisis telephone counselling, information and
referral service for ongoing community support. You are counselled by
trained volunteers on 131114.

National Association for Loss and Grief (NALAG)
NALAG's main aim is to encourage and promote professional and
community education in loss and grief. It is not a grief-counselling

organisation but it will provide useful suggestions and referrals to people seeking help.

NALAG NSW   Phone: (02) 6882 9222
NALAG VIC   Phone: (03) 9650 3000, 1800 100 023

A Hard Call
PAUL MCCANN

Day after day the same thought constantly keeps
Running through my head,
Is this child that we are having still alive or is this child dead?
Destiny of the unknown is a reality still to come.
It's a hard call to answer as the hope of life starts
To go numb.
I am like a ship tossed at sea but calm
In the eye of a storm.
As miscarriage came God did reclaim life of our
Child unborn.
Grief for the life in a womb and a tomb,
Brief the time it was there.
The gift in our hearts will never depart,
That's a blessing we share.

Chapter 3

Why me?

Wanting to start a family of your own and not conceiving as quickly, or naturally, as you might have expected can be something that a couple will face. With the average age of Australian women having their first baby now standing at 30, the issue of infertility is becoming more common. Considering the possibility of infertility or difficulty in conceiving a baby brings into play a number of options to consider, such as Assisted Reproduction Technology (ART), fertility surgery or In Vitro Fertilisation (IVF). A part of considering the options of how to deal with infertility is also making the decision as to when to stop medical treatments and consider other options for having children, such as adoption or surrogacy, or adjusting to a life without children.

Facing infertility

When a couple sets out to have a baby, they are filled with hopes, excitement, wishes and the usual fears about becoming parents. When getting pregnant doesn't come as easily or quickly as expected, feelings of grief or loss or regret can come into play. It can be difficult to manage these feelings and sometimes the focus on falling pregnant can become quite intense and all consuming. These kinds of reactions can range anywhere from normal reactions to the uncertainty about falling pregnant to intensely yearning to become pregnant.

Not only are there the physical effects and outcomes of not falling pregnant, there are also the emotional aspects that will arise and make dealing with not becoming pregnant difficult. Infertility has a strong impact on self-esteem. Suddenly your life, which may have been well planned and successful, seems out of control.

Medical treatment for infertility

One of the most challenging aspects of the infertility experience is dealing with the ups and downs relating to medical treatment and the uncertainty of the outcome. There is also the challenge of deciding when 'enough is enough'. It is important to learn how to take care of yourself, make sure that you get the support you need and manage your emotions so that your outlook remains as positive as possible.

Women will have very different responses to infertility. Some women may feel angry and frustrated at not being able to have children and others might feel guilty or to blame if their body is not doing what they expected it to do. In some instances, women can feel that they have no control over their body and that this is spilling into their everyday life. Some women may also find it difficult to be around children or resent pregnant women.

Choosing medical treatment to deal with infertility brings another set of challenges in that a woman feels that her life is on hold, yet strongly dictated by the different stages in the infertility treatment. The idea of falling pregnant naturally is controlled by the very precise monitoring of a woman's cycle along with invasive medical procedures, such as injections, ultrasound scans and possibly surgery. It is an extremely emotional time and a woman can feel that she is hopeful one minute, despairing the next.

With medical intervention, men can feel isolated from the 'conception' because the focus of the treatment is about the woman and her cycle. If the problem of conceiving is due to male infertility, some men can feel less like a man.

Alternative treatments for infertility
Alternative or natural treatments for infertility are suitable for those who are not comfortable with conventional fertility treatment or medications. People who have not had success with IVF may choose to try alternative therapies. These treatments include acupuncture, homeopathy, naturopathy, herbs, reflexology, cranial osteopathy and stress management. These treatments can also be long term and the rate of success will depend on how the individual responds to the treatment. Natural therapies can also be used in conjunction with conventional IVF to support the fertility cycle and strengthen the immune system and health of the woman undergoing the treatment.

As men and women deal in different ways with infertility, the relationship between a couple can become strained and it is important for each of the partners to remain supportive and to keep communicating with each other.

If IVF, medical intervention or alternative therapies prove not to be a solution to a couple's infertility then they need to look at options outside of having children who are biologically theirs.

Life without children

For some women and their partners, there will sadly come a time when they make the decision to stop their efforts to have a baby. While some may be trying to complete their family, for others this means stopping their attempts to have their first child.

Thinking of facing life without children or without completing your family can raise many new questions and can be quite a confusing and emotional time. These questions can range from what to do in your spare time to what to do with the rest of your life. Sometimes these issues and questions cannot be resolved without the help of a counsellor, however, most couples do learn to adapt and live a creative and fulfilling life with each other, even if it is not necessarily how they had visualised their future together.

Coming to terms with not having children can give you the ability to regain control of your life as a couple again. Infertility often leaves people in a holding pattern as they wait to fall pregnant or undergo treatment. A life without children might be difficult to think about but it does allow you to reconnect with your partner and work on goals and dreams that can be achieved together.

There is no right way of coping with infertility. It is important to allow you and your partner to have time to accept that children may not be a part of your future. There will be times when it is easier to accept and manage this than others. Continue to express your feelings and emotions with your partner. Think about how you have survived together and how your relationship with your partner can get stronger. It is a time to think about what you want for yourself.

Moving on from the dream of having children does not happen instantly. It is a journey that involves changing a mindset and building a new life with a different focus.

Lexy's story

Lexy Hamilton-Smith is a well-respected journalist and broadcaster, currently working at Channel 10 in Brisbane.

Lexy had married a man who already had three young children so they delayed having a child together until Lexy was in her mid-thirties. It took her a couple of years to get pregnant with Laurel, their miracle baby conceived naturally.

After experiencing the incredible joys and the emotional ups and downs with the birth of Laurel, they found it difficult falling pregnant again. Lexy and her husband, Dave, discovered that they had an infertility problem because of his diabetes. The next step they took was IVF.

I had a fairly high-powered job and had already tried for two years to have a baby; so you're already going through that whole process of wondering why [I wasn't falling pregnant].

Going through IVF was difficult, involving dealing with feelings of anger and resentment but also feeling that she couldn't really talk about how she felt to others. The ups and downs of an IVF cycle took its toll.

[During one cycle of IVF] I happened to have a period and I realised at that moment, I've failed, *and I just cried and cried.*

I was so devastated I could not move, but I was hosting Today Tonight *and expected to be at work.*

I couldn't tell my producer what was going on, I didn't feel I could share an incredibly personal journey with someone who I felt wouldn't understand. I went to work, had to get my hair and make-up done, I had to get briefed about the show. I had to put on an incredibly brave face and present half an hour of television.

During the course of the IVF treatment, Lexy found that she was becoming more erratic – she found the whole procedure overwhelming and distressing, with her hormones and moods running out of control. Fortunately she was able to share some of her feelings and let some of her female colleagues know what she was going through.

She also found herself experiencing extreme emotions while on IVF, something that was unexpected and very difficult to cope with.

[While I was waiting to fall pregnant on IVF] I had a lot of anger and hostility and resentment for people who were having babies, and I found that really hard to battle. I became quite resentful and angry, and probably not very nice to be with. You're thinking, Why? This isn't fair . . .

With an IVF cycle, you're not ever really pregnant and so not being pregnant doesn't entitle you to talk about it. From the moment you start that process, you're trying to create a life, which is one of the most precious things you can do in the world. You feel like you don't have any friends or family who understand, someone who's been through it.

You have a right to grieve when you have a stillborn baby and you have a right to grieve with a miscarriage, because you've told people and it's been a celebration that then becomes tragic. You get flowers and you get people patting you and hugging you and calling you. But with IVF, when do you have a right to grieve about that? Because, you know, it's two weeks, four weeks, six weeks, waiting for the phone call, waiting for the cells to divide, waiting not to get your period, when you realise, Oh my God, *at what point can you celebrate creating a life? At what point are you allowed to grieve for the loss that you feel? I never felt I had a right at all to grieve, so my sadness and tears were overwhelming . . .*

Lexy found that listening to the stories of other women going through IVF made her realise that all women deal with the treatment differently but there was still the same heartache and desperation at trying to become pregnant, and learning to cope with what was essentially controlling people's lives. It also made her realise how isolated women feel as they are losing babies or not falling pregnant and have no one to talk to.

I found it very difficult to find people to relate to. You just felt people didn't understand, and I can only imagine with a stillbirth or other loss that it would be similar. But unless you have actually lost a baby, I guess you can't begin to imagine the heartache that a woman goes through.

When you sit in the fertility clinic and you start to talk to these strangers, and they say, 'Well, I'm on my ninth time' and 'I'm on my 17th time', you think, Oh my God.

I actually didn't realise how common IVF was until I finally was able to talk about it and then I discovered there were a lot of women, even at my local school, they've never talked about it. I suddenly wasn't alone.

I think this is an issue that we do need to talk about.

Facing infertility means changing one's hopes and dreams and adjusting to what is happening in the present.

It is also about dealing with the possibility of not having children and focusing on life without them around. As Lexy clearly explains:

My dream was to have three or four children, and that's what my journey was to be, but I have three lovely stepchildren and I've got some grandchildren now, through my husband's older son who just had twins. That said, I do feel like the most blessed woman in the world that I've been able to share that journey of motherhood.

Lexy had to deal with the disappointment of not being able to have another child and she found that this was also difficult for people to understand, particularly when she already had a child through natural conception.

If you have a child, people say, 'You're okay, you've got one child, you know.'

I found that made me feel more empty . . . once I had experienced the joy of having a baby and being a mother, I felt empty not being able to do it again.

How could you explain that feeling to people because they would say, 'You are greedy, why do you want more than one child?' That's true, but inside, the heartache was worse, because I knew how wonderful it was.

Dave's condition deteriorated, which gave her a reason to rationalise why she couldn't have another child. It also made her think quite deeply about the reasons why certain things in life don't happen.

I'm a single parent, you know, a widow. I thought, as my husband's illness got worse, I was always looking for a reason why I didn't have more babies. I just thought that's the reason why, for me to cope with where my life is. I can cope really well as a parent of one; maybe I wouldn't have coped as a single parent of two or four?

It does make you search. You start thinking about your own spirituality when you can't conceive and why human life can't be formed.

You can't take anything for granted. I started to really re-evaluate and think about those things I had taken for granted. I never thought I wouldn't be able to conceive for whatever reason whether it was through my husband's ill health or because I'd left it too late.

I don't regret the IVF path because it's made me a lot more loving, I guess, particularly of children. I'm babysitting the grand-children and I'm terrific at it.

Talking to others made the infertility path and the issues associated with it much easier to help Lexy deal with things. She also found that there was a wellspring of emotion from women wanting to share their stories and just talk about their experiences.

I was finally able to confront the issue and talk about it and I got an incredible reaction from women, because it is so common . . . people don't realise that you're human, that we have just as much heartache and pain as a lot of other people.

I often get women ringing me up and they want to share their story and I feel really blessed that I can help them with that part of the journey. I feel quite comfortable about talking about it and I like listening to their stories. I don't care how long they take to tell me because I know how important it is.

Grief is an important part of the process, with grief comes an acceptance of how things are rather than how things could have been, which can help people find some inner peace with their situation.

And for me, with the loss of my husband, I found the grieving had been for all of those losses. I'm in a good place and I'm able to talk about all these things now, and I can help other women cope with this issue.

You know the tears that flood your eyes as you face the unexplainable, Why me, why didn't this work? *I mean that's life, it's a journey of joy and sadness and somehow we all have to learn to cope with that and move on.*

Lexy believes that it is important for people to be more compassionate towards women suffering infertility or the loss of a baby.

It's okay to be sad and it's okay to give someone a hug . . . a random hug, and it's okay to let a woman talk about their overwhelming sadness.

They are silent tears, no one hears and no one sees. You lock yourself away. Ultimately, it is about the change of the culture, we need a cultural shift because more and more people have to use science to conceive and yet, as a society, we don't deal with that very well.

Deb and Geoff's story

Deb and Geoff have suffered multiple miscarriages and have also gone down the IVF path. Their story shows how a couple deals with the stress of IVF and the waiting for the call to say the embryo has taken and how they maintained the strength and communication in their relationship, despite the difficulties in conceiving. Deb is also a trained grief counsellor with the Bonnie Babes Foundation on the Gold Coast.

We started trying to have a baby in 1998 and we lost our first baby at eight weeks in October 1999 and then couldn't get pregnant again; we tried for three years. I was diagnosed with polycystic ovarian syndrome and we ended up on the IVF program and we were lucky enough to get pregnant on the first try; at 17 weeks we lost our twins, Joel and Emma, they were born two days apart and then again we couldn't get pregnant.

We did two more IVF cycles but couldn't get pregnant and we got to the stage where we thought we would never fall pregnant.

Deb became pregnant naturally with their son Hunter but the same thing happened as with their other babies, bleeding at eight weeks and then waters breaking at 19 weeks. They lost Hunter. As both Geoff and Deb felt they weren't coping, they contacted Bonnie Babes and found that sharing some of this grief and experience eased the burden for them. They were at a turning point in their relationship with the stress and strain providing too much to work through on their own. Luckily they were one of the few couples who didn't separate or divorce and managed to endure the pain of the loss together. Many couples do separate with the stress of dealing with miscarriage and stillbirth.

The unpredictable outcome of an IVF cycle can cause stress and may also trigger feelings of depression, particularly while waiting for the two weeks leading up to the pregnancy test after implantation. This waiting can feel like a lifetime for many couples and also cause anxiety as they become intensely attuned to what is happening with the woman's body – any twinge, sensation or unusual feeling may feel threatening. Deb found the procedure of IVF okay to deal with but the waiting was dreadful for her.

. . . the worst part was from when the embryo was put back in and waiting until you found out whether you were pregnant or not – two weeks . . .

I had a girlfriend where they told her that by a certain time they'll ring if it's positive and then, if they don't ring, you ring . . .

she literally sits there in front of the clock, because she always goes in to work on the day, so the day will go faster . . . and she's sitting there and she's waiting for that phone call . . .

Deb and Geoff bravely echo the sentiments of many couples who have trouble falling pregnant or are going through yet another IVF cycle.

. . . you think terrible things . . . you see a pregnant woman walking down the street, you think, I hope your baby dies like mine did *. . . I remember the first time, I thought,* I can't believe I'm thinking this. I'm the most horrible person in the whole world. *I've spoken to other women since then and they're like: 'Oh . . . thank God, you know, I thought it was just me.'*

Even though Deb and Geoff are still grieving for their babies they find it a comfort to know that other people are going through similar experiences and that they are learning, in their own way and in their own time, to deal with their grief. They have learnt to ignore to other people's expectations of when they should stop grieving.

Salik's story

Salik has a great career working across the globe in film and TV commercial production. Being in control of his working life didn't translate when it came to trying for a child.

Andee, my wife, was already in her forties, and we decided that we would try and have children. We were very lucky. We had a wonderful doctor who specialised in women over 40 wanting to have children. We went through IVF. Andee also had other problems which signalled that not only falling pregnant but keeping the pregnancy would be difficult. Our first miscarriage was an absolute shock.

Andee and Salik kept trying and after five miscarriages, baby Stella went the full distance. Andee's health complications meant that Stella would be their only child.

Martine's story

This is a brave letter that Martine wrote to herself about her feelings of being unable to hold on to her pregnancies. This honest account gives an insight into what goes through the minds of many women who have suffered through multiple miscarriages.

[Written just after Martine's fourth miscarriage]

Today it's just numbness. I'm not crying and wonder why. Is it possible I'm getting used to this grief. Can a person really get used to losing babies? Is it possible to become blasé? This time I feel as though I never was pregnant. My symptoms simply vanished with the first spot. I knew it was all over from that moment. Not a shred of hope. I don't think it's right that I'm not crying. I'm scared.

This time I knew. The doctor invited me to look at the screen so that I could be sure in my mind. I declined.

For the first time the potential reality of never having a child is beginning to gnaw at me. A simmering hysteria that will erupt if I think too hard about it. I must keep it hidden, wedged into the back of my mind but it builds and builds to a lump in my throat. Swallowing doesn't help.

What will life be without a family? What will I do with the rest of my life? There is no greater purpose in my mind than to create a family. To eventually have grandchildren. What sort of selfish life am I heading into, a life of continuous lattes and trips to Ikea . . .

Martine finally had a baby girl, Phoebe, at the end of 2007.

Learning to cope with infertility

Infertility can be a devastating shock to a couple but it is important to realise that it is not only a physical condition, it also affects people emotionally – in very different ways. Understanding that people cope differently with infertility helps to accept that individual reactions are normal. Identifying the positives of your situation and how you are coping will help you deal with the stress and grieving that may be felt.

Live for the present

- Make the most of the resources you have. Think about your situation now and recognise the positives of life rather than thinking about how much of a difference having a child will make to your life. You may not be pregnant but think about the things that you do have, the things that you enjoyed doing before trying to fall pregnant. Devote time and attention to your partner or to others who may need your help.

Gathering information

- If you are involved in a fertility treatment, make sure that you are well-informed and empowered by the knowledge you have to assist you in falling pregnant and also by being aware of what can happen if pregnancy does not occur.

Understand the emotions associated with infertility

- Become familiar with the emotional stages that you may go through during infertility. These stages can include denial, shock, anger, guilt, sadness and grief, and these feelings can occur in any order. Remind yourself that these feelings are normal and you have a right to feel them during this time.

Finding support

- Infertility can be lonely and isolating, but it doesn't have to be. Support is available from many sources, such as your general practitioner or health professional. There are also online support groups, chat rooms and counselling available. Find a supportive social network to help you get through difficult times.

Communicating with your partner

- Emotional support from your partner is very important. Ask your partner how you can support him or her, and tell them what kind of emotional support you need. Think of ways to nurture your relationship and make it your number one priority. Be aware of each other's emotional responses to stressful situations.

Setting achievable goals that are not related to having children

- Think and plan for things that you can do as a couple, such as travelling or long-term plans of sharing the future together, rather than putting your life on hold waiting to fall pregnant.

Common Questions

What is infertility and when should I seek medical help?

Most experts define infertility as not being able to get pregnant after at least one year of trying. Women who are able to get pregnant but then have repeated miscarriages may also be said to be infertile.

Most healthy women under the age of 30 shouldn't worry about infertility unless they've been trying to get pregnant for at least a year. At this point, women should talk to their doctors about a fertility evaluation. Men should also talk to their doctors if this much time has passed.

In some cases, women should talk to their doctors sooner. Women in their thirties who've been trying to get pregnant for six months should speak to their doctors as soon as possible. A woman's chances of having a baby decrease rapidly every year after the age of 30, so getting a complete and timely fertility evaluation is especially important.

How does age affect fertility?

From the age of 30, the per month chance of conception is a little over 20 per cent. By the age of 36 a woman's chance of conceiving per month decreases to 15 per cent. The downward slope continues until about age 45 with the average natural fertility rate per month being approximately one per cent.

What causes infertility?

There are many reasons why a couple may not be able to conceive naturally. After a woman's age, male infertility is the biggest single factor.

Other causes of infertility might include ovulation disorders, tubal disease, endometriosis, and a combination of male and female reproductive issues.

What are the options for treating infertility?

There are a number of medical options for treating infertility. It is best to talk to your health professional to seek advice on the steps to take to deal with the infertility and also work out what is causing the infertility.

There are also non-traditional medical treatments, naturopathic or holistic treatments some couples can consider trying. Couples may also seek counselling if there is no medical reason as it may be a psychological issue.

When do I decide to stop the fertility treatments and think about other options?

Some couples decide that as much as they want to have a baby, they won't go to extreme measures or pursue invasive fertility treatments. Others spend years and thousands of dollars exhausting all of their options.

No one can tell you when to stop trying to conceive – that's a decision you need to make with your partner and your health professional. You need to think about how far you are willing to go to get pregnant and if you only want a biological child rather than looking at the option of adoption or fostering. Some couples experience a clear moment when they make their decision, others may find themselves changing their decision several times, revisiting it as their feelings shift. This is a normal and understandable part of the process.

Resources

Access – infertility

ACCESS Australia is a consumer-based, independent, non-profit organisation committed to being the national voice in promoting the wellbeing and welfare of infertile people of all ages.

www.access.org.au

To Baby Daniel From Dad
WAYNE

To my little baby Daniel who died not long after birth. He took his last breath in my arms. What can I say? I feel a pain, an emptiness in my heart I cannot describe. You came into our lives after we tried for so long for a baby and then you were gone. Mummy planted a tree at the end of the garden. I sat in your nursery many nights and cried. I often send a prayer to God to keep you safe.

I wish we could have had longer together. You will always be sadly missed and loved. I will remember your little face and small hands and toes forever.

I love you, Daniel.
Your Daddy.

Chapter 4

What went wrong?

There has been a death in the family
No eulogy, no coffin
No funeral, no black
And yet, there has been a death in the family
No undertaker, no hearse
No cemetery, no grave
And yet, there has been a death in the family
No belly, no fullness
No lifeline, no baby
There has been a death in the family.

Helen Warner Smith

A miscarriage is the loss of a pregnancy before the baby has reached 20 weeks (this figure may vary in some countries between 20 to 24 weeks) of development at which life outside the womb is possible.

In Australia today, one in four pregnancies ends in a loss, with the majority lost very early, often before the woman knows she is pregnant.

Miscarriage is a complex biological and psychological event, representing the loss of a desired and loved child. For the majority of babies who are lost through miscarriage, it will not be possible to identify a cause or reason for the loss. This is extremely frustrating for parents who yearn for some explanation for the death of their child. While many risk factors have been identified in early pregnancy, most causal factors are beyond the voluntary control of families affected by such losses.

It is estimated that 1 per cent of couples trying to conceive will experience recurrent pregnancy loss, defined by three or more consecutive losses. While all women who experience the trauma of a recurrent pregnancy loss should seek investigations under the guidance of their obstetrician, unfortunately a treatable cause can only be identified in about 30 per cent of cases. In spite of this, 75 per cent of couples with a history of recurrent loss will experience a successful subsequent pregnancy.

There is still a great deal not known about the many possible reasons for miscarriage and it is usually difficult to identify a cause. Some of the main factors and causes are listed. Miscarriages are usually due to a combination of causes rather than a single one.

Chromosomal abnormalities
When a sperm and an egg join to create an embryo, an incredible amount of matching occurs between the mother's and father's genetic material. Chromosomal abnormalities occur in the child when there is an anomaly in this process, for example, trisomy (three copies of a particular chromosome) occurs with chromosome 21, in Down syndrome.

When a significant chromosomal abnormality is present, the affected embryo may activate a genetic program which signals for miscarriage to occur.

Genetic studies have determined that at least 50 per cent of babies who are miscarried in the first trimester (i.e. in the first 12 weeks) had a significant chromosomal abnormality, making it the commonest cause of miscarriage. Currently these abnormalities cannot be prevented, reversed or cured by any known medical therapy. Progress into understanding the basis of these abnormalities and how they may be prevented is difficult.

Blighted ovum
There is a sac but not embryo inside it, either because no embryo formed or the embryo stopped growing very early. Eventually, this results in a miscarriage. 'Blighted ovum' is an older term but one that is still used; the preferred term is 'early fetal demise'.

Incomplete implantation
After an embryo has been formed, it needs to implant in the lining of the womb where the placenta will grow and nourish the baby during pregnancy. Sometimes this process may not be successful and the child cannot gain enough nutrients to survive. Difficulties with implantation are associated with uterine abnormalities such as a separate uterus or uterine fibroids.

Infection
There are some bacteria and viruses that can be harmful to the baby as well as the mother. In some instances these

infections are the cause of miscarriage. Examples of this include listeria, toxoplasmosis and rubella. Fortunately, with the high standard of antenatal care in Australia, these complications are increasingly uncommon.

Endocrine problems
There are a number of disorders of the endocrine system which may contribute to pregnancy loss, including:

- Poorly controlled thyroid disease
- Poorly controlled diabetes/gestational diabetes
- Polycystic ovarian syndrome
- Obesity

Specific treatments are available for each of these medical conditions.

Immune system problems
There are a number of auto-immune conditions which have been associated with miscarriage and recurrent pregnancy loss, the most common of these is known as the 'antiphospholipid syndrome'. This syndrome occurs when the mother's immune system responds abnormally to some of the factors in the bloodstream, which causes the placenta to develop abnormally. There are also other immune abnormalities that contribute to miscarriage, with the baby being rejected.

Blood-clotting disorders
These types of disorders include a number of conditions where various blood clotting factors are either absent or present in extreme levels. These types of conditions cause clotting problems that affect the developing baby without

necessarily causing medical problems or symptoms in the mother.

Cervical incompetence
In this condition, the cervix begins to shorten before the onset of labour, usually between 17 to 19 weeks. This can often be prevented by an operation where a stitch is placed in the cervix to strengthen it and prevent it opening before time.

Placental abruption
This condition occurs when the normally formed placenta begins to break away from the wall of the womb too early. It can occur at any stage after 20 weeks of pregnancy and affects 1 per cent of all pregnancies, causing problems such as premature deliveries.

Lifestyle factors
There are a number of general physical health and lifestyle factors, which have been associated with an increased risk of miscarriage and stillbirth. Many of these factors can be changed once pregnancy is confirmed. These factors include cigarette smoking, alcohol consumption, illicit drug use and a very high caffeine intake.

Experiencing a miscarriage
It is extremely common to experience some type of light bleeding during the first trimester of a pregnancy. When this unexplained bleeding occurs during the first 20 weeks of pregnancy it is referred to as 'threatened miscarriage'; more than half of these pregnancies continue normally.

The symptoms of a miscarriage include heavy bleeding and painful cramping, feeling weak or experiencing chills or a high temperature. Always contact your doctor or midwife as soon as possible. If large clots or tissue is being passed or there is pain then it is important to go to your nearest hospital emergency department. A doctor or midwife will give you a brief check-up to see if the cervix is closed. An open cervix indicates that a miscarriage is unavoidable at this point in the pregnancy. This is the physical experience of a miscarriage. If the cervix is closed, an ultrasound is done to check for an ectopic (outside the womb) pregnancy.

The emotional experience of a miscarriage is different for everyone, depending on what your baby means to you, how you feel about it, and the supportive system you have around you. Most women who have suffered a miscarriage feel a sadness and regret, along with shock and confusion as their minds try to make sense of what is happening to their bodies. Some women feel angry, some feel guilty and blame themselves as they try to make sense of why the miscarriage happened. There also may be feelings of emptiness, stress, panic and an overwhelming sense of losing control.

The physical and emotional aftermath

In some miscarriages, the uterus empties itself spontaneously. In some cases, though, the baby dies but is not miscarried, or some pregnancy tissue is left behind. If so, the doctor may suggest a dilation and curettage (D&C) to surgically remove the material. Other treatments include medical management, which is the prescription of pills to start the miscarriage process. Some women can choose to let the miscarriage happen naturally. Around 80 per cent of women will not need surgical intervention, although some of these will go ahead with the procedure to 'get it over with'. The amount of bleeding and pain varies but can depend on the size of the pregnancy and the way the miscarriage is managed. Physical symptoms relating to emotional loss can sometimes be felt in many ways – feeling very tired, experiencing headaches or stomach-aches, insomnia. Always speak to your health professional if these symptoms become a concern.

After a miscarriage, you grieve for a person you never knew, and for a relationship that ended before it really began. You grieve for the loss of your future as a parent of the baby who has died. Sometimes it is difficult to grieve for the baby, as there is no tangible evidence of your baby's existence. There is usually no baby to see, hold, touch, no funeral and no memories to keep. Friends, family and healthcare providers may consider the miscarriage as just a minor event, not even a loss. Because often no one recognises or acknowledges the extent of your loss, you may feel you need to discount or disregard your feelings of loss and grief as they arise.

Your feelings can seem overwhelming, and you may find yourself experiencing a range of emotions. Some people want to talk about their experience; others prefer to keep to themselves. Your partner will also be suffering but might be grieving in a very different way. Male partners sometimes feel powerless to help and feel that they haven't been able to protect their partner from such a devastating physical and emotional loss. *Chapter 2 – Understanding grief, guilt and loss* will help you cope with the grief that comes with a miscarriage and the early loss of a baby.

Trying to fall pregnant again

People's feelings do vary after the experience of pregnancy loss. You may feel that you want to get pregnant as quickly as possible, or you may feel anxious at the thought of going through another pregnancy and dealing with the potential of more heartache. Most importantly, discussion between partners considering another pregnancy is key to helping with the decision.

It is natural when trying to fall pregnant after a miscarriage that a couple aim to do whatever they can to give their next pregnancy the best possible chance of success. There are no hard and fast rules but it is important that the emotional and physical health of both parents is good. It is also important that you give yourself the time that you need to recover physically and emotionally, and to not feel pressurised by family and friends.

Most health professionals advise waiting until you have had at least one period after the miscarriage before trying to conceive again, however, there is no evidence that the length of time until you conceive again will increase or decrease the risk of miscarrying in the next pregnancy. It is important to have an overall health check-up to make sure all is well before falling pregnant again.

Clare's story

Clare has been a midwife since 1992. She established the
position of pregnancy loss coordinator at the hospital
she worked at to help women who were suffering
pregnancy loss and needed support while they were in
hospital. Clare's story is interesting as she is able to look
at miscarriage from both sides – as a midwife and as a
woman who has experienced the early loss of a baby.
Clare has also been a grief counsellor with the Bonnie
Babes Foundation for over ten years.

As a midwife, Clare found that her role was to make
women who suffered a loss feel a little more in control
of the situation. She would encourage bereaved parents to
make the best of the situation by thinking about how to
remember their lost baby. She stresses that communication
is very important to help with the grieving process.

*I guess I always thought my role was to make the situation
as best as possible, not that you can change it, but give as many
memories and celebrate the life of this baby when it was alive.*

*You communicate with the parents about their needs and
try to accommodate what they want even if it isn't quite black
and white.*

Clare's role became even more poignant as she struggled
with multiple miscarriages of her own. Even though she
dealt with grieving parents on a daily basis, she still had
a difficult time when it came to her own loss, despite all
the experience and knowledge she had as a midwife. With
her first miscarriage she rationalised that she was part of
the one in four statistic, not that it made it any easier for
her and her partner to cope.

But when it happened a second time, it was really quite devastating and I was left wondering, is this going to keep happening with my future outcomes? I took time off work and my husband did the same. He found that friends were quite supportive, they would ask him how he was, not only how I was, which was good.

Clare also came to realise how differently men and women grieve and how they adapt to the situation. A miscarriage can place intense strain on a relationship.

Males and females grieve at different stages, but often the women would say, 'He doesn't care, he's gotten over this, he's gone back to work, he's playing golf . . .'

I found with the first couple of weeks, my husband was the one grieving and I was the one supporting him, then when he moved on from that stage I was able to fall in a big heap.

That's the way men cope. Generally, women would take time off work and have that time to themselves and grieve. I don't know what response men would get if they decided not to go to work. I think it's important to recognise fathers in this process.

Grieving took time and Clare mentions that the pace that people grieve varies from person to person.

My boss was ringing me up and asking when I was coming back to work. Who are they to judge when I'm ready to come back to work? Yes, there is a point where you have to get on with life and sitting at home isn't healthy, but hopefully you know within yourself. Everyone is different when they grieve.

Trying for another baby after a miscarriage was traumatic and Clare took a number of precautions to try to alleviate her fears of miscarrying again.

I had testing after the second miscarriage. Because it took us over a year to get pregnant the first time, then we lost it at three months. *Going through the third pregnancy, I was beside myself, I had three to four ultrasounds.*

From her hospital experience, Clare understood all too well the fragility of conceiving and carrying a child to full-term, and what the loss of a baby can mean for a couple's idea of the future.

. . . from past experience women think once they get past the 12 weeks they're relieved, but it's not all good then. You put so much planning into it with dreams and hopes, work out the dates they go to school – and then it all comes crashing down.

Clare stresses the importance of communication and how it has helped her with not only her personal situation but has made her have more empathy in her working life.

You feel like you're the only one at the time; when you do get over that initial grieving time it's good to know there are people out there who you can talk to and understand, and have a group designed just for pregnancy loss alone. It's recognition that you have gone through something quite terrible.

With my own miscarriages, you think your good friends are the ones supporting you, but people come out of the woodwork. Women are probably good that way that they can bring things into the open and have a good talk about things.

Mara's story

Mara has worked as the editor of *Practical Parenting* magazine in the UK and currently works as Editor for the magazine in Australia. In her career, she has seen it all in respect to parent and child issues.

At 25, I tried to have kids (after years of trying not to get pregnant) and ended up getting pregnant easily. My husband and I wanted to have babies because we were so in love.

But I was spotting at ten weeks, then full-on bleeding, and I ended up in hospital. The midwives said, 'Nothing is there, there's no baby there.' The clinical callousness was stunning! They asked, 'Are you sure you're pregnant?' This was after all my tests and confirmations.

As with many women, Mara believed that becoming pregnant at such a young age, things would be fairly straightforward. She was unprepared as to how much she and her husband would grieve.

It was the first time I'd seen my husband Anthony cry.

I was put in a ward with pregnant women (and others waiting for a hysterectomy). I was crying silently. At 25 I was having trouble having kids. It wasn't like I was 40, I thought. It put doubts in my head. I thought there was something wrong with me and that we may never have children.

But we're glass half full people, so we tried again. After six months, we had a positive test. Our other friends were all having healthy babies, but we felt very aware of potential problems. Acquaintances would say: 'If it turns out all right . . .' Other people said, 'Fingers crossed.'

Mara held the pregnancy until 12 weeks but the same thing happened. She started bleeding and lost the baby.

Adding to the shock was the possibility that any leftover cells from the pregnancy could possibly be cancerous.

I had to get all the cells scraped away as there was a chance they could be malignant — if any were left in my uterus I might need chemotherapy. How can this happen to me when we were simply trying to have a baby?

I felt like a loser. Anthony and I decided to go backpacking in Europe for six months. We decided that if we were unable to have kids, we may as well spend our money on ourselves.

On a Greek island we had a teary conversation about our losses and decided to try again for a baby. I was six weeks pregnant again by the time we returned home to Australia. That baby girl is now ten years old!

Maybe the message is, 'Ignore your problems, change your life and it will work out.' Who knows? I still don't really know what the problem was with me.

After her experience with miscarriage, Mara realised that there were many women who had suffered the heartbreak of miscarriage. It was something that no one ever talked about openly but once the issue was raised, the floodgates opened.

As editor of Practical Parenting, *I have learned that whenever we mentioned miscarriage, a staggering number of women came and talked about their losses.*

I was sent two roses by a reader when I wrote that I'd had two miscarriages. Another reader told me the story that she'd had one unwanted pregnancy — then nine miscarriages when she actually wanted children.

Many people think miscarriage is a 'sad issue', so it's swept under the carpet. Sad stories scare readers, apparently. There can be pressure not to write about miscarriage in parenting magazines.

It's actually an integral part of the whole process for some women; the whole journey of becoming a parent.

My miscarriages weren't babies; they were hopes, plans for the future and dreams of our family.

Beatrice's story

Beatrice is a young mum with an active two-year-old. At the time of sharing her story, she was expecting her second child.

Miscarriage was just a word to me. No one I knew had had a problem. I thought I was invincible. Then I had my first, Owen. We even bought a double pram because we wanted two close together.

At 13 weeks, I was bleeding. I told my mum and my husband. I went to hospital and they said, 'It's okay'. I was told to take it easy . . . I was worse the next day. The hospital did an ultrasound.

The baby had been dead for a couple of weeks. My husband started looking sick. It was the worst moment in my life. I asked, 'What's the sex?' It was too young, they couldn't tell. No support was offered. I went into myself. I didn't want to talk to anyone for weeks. The comments followed, 'It might be for the best', 'There's no reason.'

I fell pregnant again five months later. I was wary but the statistics said things should be okay. From 10 weeks, I became worried whenever I went to the toilet. My husband was too. We lost that baby together.

I felt like I was only ever going to have the one child. I realised how lucky I'd been having no problems with the first. I started resenting other pregnant women or news of other people having babies.

My husband, Thomas, shut off from the world. He didn't want a shoulder to lean on, or sympathy. It's hard to grieve and support others at the same time, going to work and pretending to move on.

I couldn't deal with my family. You become angry at the world.

I don't know how people deal with a child dying at full-term. I wouldn't know what to say if a friend had a miscarriage, nothing can make the pain go away. Nobody understands, your emotions are so extreme. Some days I couldn't lift my head out of bed. I was nasty to my husband until he told me it was just as bad a pain for him, but he still had to keep a brave face.

Even now I blame myself. What did I do wrong? Something I drank? Something I lifted? The flea treatment I gave the dog?

I'd given up on getting pregnant — I haven't told anyone, not even Mum, but I'm currently at 25 weeks. And so paranoid, I didn't want to jinx it by telling people. I'm having nightmares. I freak out if I can't feel kicking. I conceived this one after a Bonnie Babes charity event (National Babies Day). I wonder if I am setting myself up for another heartbreak?

The way I see it, the more research the more answers. It's all very well saying that it must be Nature's way, but it would be nice to know more about what causes miscarriages to happen.

Julian's story

Julian counts family as the most important aspect of his
life. The death of his daughter was devastatingly sad and
he'd had trouble coming to terms with it and dealing with
his feelings over his loss.

*Julian and his partner, Mel, suffered the loss of their baby a few
years ago. He was overseas when he got the call from Mel to come
home. After a 30-hour flight he made it back to be by Mel's side
in hospital.*

*They [the medical staff] were saying that the baby's heartbeat
was quite irregular and the baby wasn't developing. We went to
the hospital and did all that sort of stuff and checked ourselves
in and Melanie was induced. This little person came out; at 20
weeks she was still big enough to hold with both hands.*

*We named her Carly Jane, and that was probably a good thing
in that way we embraced her life for the short period. She was a
person. And then they cremated her a few days later. We have a
little urn with her at home.*

*Everyone does deal with it differently, and I know Mel and
I probably dealt with it a lot differently. I think I was 30 and
she was 22 in the year when we got married, so there was quite
an age difference, and life was a bit different for both of us from
that point on.*

Julian found it hard to cope with people not fully
acknowledging his grief and that Carly Jane was a little
person and he was her father.

*I still remember what she looked like. I think probably the
hardest thing to deal with was not getting the recognition that
this was a person. We lost a daughter and I am still frustrated*

we couldn't get a birth certificate [because she was under the gestation period that is legally recognised as a birth].

Unfortunately the grief and differences between Julian and his partner had an effect on their relationship but he believes he has come to terms with his grief.

Mel is my ex-wife now, but I still love her for what she had to go through. It is not the easiest thing.

I think it's like anything in life, when you are happy, be really happy, if you are grieving, maybe better to grieve more and get it out. Hit that bottom pit and then go up. Talking about it is a good thing; it is a really good thing.

I think if this generation goes through understanding and they are able to talk about it, then maybe another generation coming through will be educated from the parents.

I found the more I actually talk about Carly, the daughter that I don't have, and that's how I refer to her; she will always be my daughter.

Tony and Carolyn's story

Tony has worked and supported causes related to grief and loss and has an understanding of what is involved with the loss of a child — on an intellectual level. This didn't prepare Tony and Carolyn for their first loss.

Tony and Carolyn fell pregnant easily. Their visit to the doctor brought them news that they didn't expect.

The thing that stays in my memory was, we were very excited. It wasn't until we went to the 11-week appointment with the obstetrician — we were pretty excited to take the first photo home. Carolyn said to me, 'Are we going to get a photo or video to take home?' I said, 'We'll see, one step at a time.'

We went in and got Carolyn all hooked up to the machine and I watched; we started looking around to find the baby and it seemed to take a while and I thought that there was something wrong. Just the way the obstetrician said, 'Oh, there's nothing here.'

He could find the sac but couldn't find a baby inside. He came up with a stat: one in four pregnancies ends in a loss.

Tony and Carolyn suddenly became one of those statistics and their excitement over the pregnancy was quickly turned around. They realised that to get through they needed to rely on the strong support of family and friends.

When that statistic is brought to your attention, you see how common it really it is. You don't know until you go through these things as you go along. All of a sudden the best learning is where you experience it yourself. People that haven't got a support network, who do they turn to?

Learning to cope with miscarriage

Dealing with the physical and emotional effects of miscarriage can be difficult but it is important to keep in mind that everyone experiences their loss and their grief differently. Mourning the loss of your baby can take time and drain your energy. Give yourself the time and space to accept your loss and gain the strength to look toward the future.

Recognise that a miscarriage is a significant and real loss
- For most couples, miscarriage is the death of a baby. Acknowledge this loss by naming your baby, giving a donation or gift to a special charity or planting a tree in memory. Even if no one else knows what you have done, this gesture can make you feel better.

Acknowledge that feelings about your loss can resurface sometime after your miscarriage

- The date the baby was due or the anniversary of the loss can be a difficult time. Talk to your partner or friends and family about how you are feeling. Find a way to commemorate your baby at these times, such as lighting a candle and having a quiet moment in remembrance.

Understand that men and women deal with miscarriage differently

- The way you express your grief is very personal and may be different from the way your partner deals with feelings. When you are both hurting, you may not be able to give and receive support as you have at other times in your life. Be patient and keep communicating.

Find a support system

- Be it friends or family or a specific social support group, even though individual circumstances are different, having a common bond can be a way of resolving feelings and preventing you from feeling isolated.

Common Questions

I feel upset and depressed. Is this normal?

Some women recover quickly, others take longer to recover emotionally. A miscarriage is a loss of a baby and the feelings of grief are natural. Don't expect too much of yourself or berate yourself for not bouncing back.

When will I stop bleeding?

This depends on the stage that you miscarried at. The further along in the pregnancy, the longer the period of bleeding and severe abdominal cramping. The bleeding and any pain will gradually become less. You are likely to get your period four to six weeks after a miscarriage. This period may be heavier than usual.

Why did I miscarry?

Even though one in four pregnancies ends in a loss, it is usually difficult to know the exact cause. It can be difficult to accept that there is no certainty as to why the miscarriage happened. A miscarriage is unlikely to have happened because of anything you did or didn't do.

Why is there no explanation?

Some babies who are miscarried are totally medically unexplained and potentially could have been as healthy as you or me and lived a long and productive life.

My husband and I had sex the night before I lost the baby. Can sex injure the baby?

Sex cannot injure the baby. If you have certain problems during pregnancy, such as the placenta being too low (placenta praevia) your doctor will tell you to avoid having sex. Unless your doctor has given you this advice, then sex is safe during pregnancy.

What can I do to remember my baby? It was a miscarriage and there was no burial.

Some things you can do to help remember your baby include the planting of a special tree, a plaque placed in the children's memorial section of the cemetery, naming a star after the child (this can be done through the International Star Registry at www.starregistry.com), writing in a journal or putting together a memory box of things you associated with your pregnancy.

I am in my forties, do I have an increased chance of miscarriage?

Women older than age 35 have a higher risk of miscarriage than younger women. After 35, every year increases the risk of miscarriage.

When should I go back to work?

This depends on how you are feeling physically and emotionally. Facing your work colleagues might be difficult and you might have trouble concentrating or you may find that the routine and focus of work to give you a sense of regaining some normality in your life.

The thought of becoming pregnant again makes me anxious. Is this normal?

Many women feel anxious about becoming pregnant and miscarrying again. Some people find it helpful to get early scans during the next pregnancy as a reassurance that the pregnancy is progressing. Talking to your health professional or your partner can help alleviate some of the anxiety.

Why is my sexual relationship with my partner so difficult after a miscarriage?

For some couples, making love is comforting and brings them close, but for others it is a reminder of the lost pregnancy. It is also common for one partner to want to make love – perhaps to show how much they care – but for the other not to want it. For women, in particular, sex can be a physical reminder of the pregnancy and the miscarriage. It is not uncommon to have problems with sex for a while. Seek help if you feel that these problems have been going on for too long or you are having trouble dealing with your feelings about sex.

Resources

The Bonnie Babes Foundation counsellors are trained to help in every aspect of pregnancy loss and a counsellor who specifically deals with miscarriage can be contacted to support you after your loss.

Suggested reading:

Borg, S. *When Pregnancy Fails*, Beacon Press, Boston, 1981

Friedman, R. *Surviving Pregnancy Loss*, Little Brown, Boston, 1982

Ilse, S. and Appelbaum, A. *Empty Arms: coping with miscarriage, stillbirth and infant death*, Wintergreen Press, 1982

Moffit, P. & Kohn, I. *Pregnancy Loss: a silent sorrow*, Routledge, US, 2000

Moulder, C. *Miscarriage: women's experiences and needs*, Routledge, UK, 1992, 2001

Nicol, M. *Loss of a Baby: understanding maternal grief*, Bantam Books, Sydney, 1989

Rank, M. *Free to Grieve: Healing and Encouragement for those who have Suffered Miscarriage and Stillbirth*, 2004

Regan, L. *Miscarriage: what everyone needs to know, a positive new approach*, Bloomsbury Publishing, 1997

Rousselot, S. *Avoiding miscarriage: everything you need to know to feel more confident in pregnancy*, Sea Change Press, US, 2006

Ryan, A. *A Silent Love: personal stories of coming to terms with miscarriage*, Penguin Books, Ringwood, Victoria, 2000

Chapter 5

A parent without a child

Stillbirth, miscarriage and neonatal death are the hardest losses to be faced with. After carrying a baby, along with the hopes, expectations and dreams of what is to come with that child, suffering a loss feels like the possibilities for what was planned in the future have gone. The intense pain of experiencing a stillbirth comes from the change from the bubbling feeling of anticipation to an intense blow of disbelief and shock. A parent-to-be waiting for that moment to become a parent becomes a parent without a child.

Stillbirth

Stillbirth is when a baby dies while it is inside its mother and can occur anytime from 20 weeks until immediately before birth. One in every 140 babies born in Australia is stillborn. In Australia each year 2,000 babies are stillborn and this number has remained steady for over ten years. That said, little information is published on stillbirth and it is only in recent years that there has been an increasing awareness of stillbirth and the possible causes.

Most stillbirths occur before labour begins. The pregnant woman may suspect something is wrong if she cannot feel her baby kicking. A number of stillbirths occur during labour and delivery. An ultrasound can confirm the death of the baby by showing that there is no longer a heartbeat.

Neonatal death

When a baby dies in the first 28 days of life, it is called neonatal death. In 2006 there were approximately 3,000 perinatal deaths (when a baby dies up to seven days after birth), with 2,100 fetal deaths (stillbirths) and 900 neonatal deaths in Australia. Neonatal death most frequently occurs as a result of prematurity when the baby is born with underdeveloped organs or a variety of other complications. Abnormalities and birth defects might minimise the baby's chances of survival. Although medical science has advanced considerably in the past decade, only a small percentage of babies born between 23 or 24 weeks gestation survive. However, some miracle babies do survive.

There is usually no single reason for stillbirth or neonatal death but several factors are often involved. The most common contributing causes are low birth weight, congenital abnormalities and specific infections that go undiagnosed, such as urinary tract or genital infections or certain viruses. Chronic health conditions in the mother can also increase the risk of stillbirth, such as high blood pressure, diabetes or kidney disease. Sometimes the placenta fails towards the end of the pregnancy, or even during labour, and on occasions the stress of the birth is too great for the baby to survive. Unfortunately, events can take a tragic turn during the birth with complications arising, such as umbilical cord accidents and abnormal placentas, resulting in the death of the baby.

Dealing with the decisions that need to be made after the loss of a child

If your baby's death has been diagnosed before delivery, options are given as to how the baby will be delivered. Some parents choose to wait for a natural labour, which usually happens around two weeks after the baby has died. If labour has not begun after two weeks, health professionals will recommend inducing labour to reduce any further health complications for the mother. Most couples choose to have labour induced soon after they learn of their baby's death.

After delivery, the baby, placenta and umbilical cord are examined to try to determine the cause of death. An autopsy is often recommended to help test for chromosomal problems or other genetic disorders. However, in up to 10 per cent of all cases, these tests cannot determine the cause of stillbirth. Some parents are not comfortable with an autopsy or their religious beliefs prohibit it and choose not to have one, however an autopsy can help with medical research to reduce the statistics of stillbirth. A variety of tests can be conducted, such as X-rays or other genetic testing.

Having a live baby diagnosed with serious problems can be something known before birth or something realised after the birth. In the case of a baby born with medical problems, the baby is sometimes taken away very quickly and separated from the parents straight after the birth. For rural families, this separation may involve hundreds of kilometres. This can be traumatic and terrifying for the parents, leaving them wondering if they will see their baby.

It is important to do what feels right for you and your partner at the time. Always voice your concerns or ask for special arrangements that will help you come to terms with your loss and to help you create a memory of your baby. This might involve being moved to a quieter room where you can spend time with your baby, or ask that your immediate family be with you.

In the difficult event of a loss, take your time to make decisions and don't try to make them on your own. Most hospital staff in the maternity ward are trained to help you make informed decisions by letting you know what options are available to you. There is no wrong or right decision, just the decision that feels right for you and your partner.

The Bonnie Babes Foundation counsellors can be contacted by phone on 1300 266 643 or can visit the hospital, too, as you go through the process. This is available in regional hospitals, too, and in all states.

Becoming a parent without a child

Stillbirths and neonatal deaths are emotional experiences. Immediately following such a birth many parents find it helpful to view their babies and to have a chance to say hello and goodbye. Hospital staff are generally more than willing to allow parents to spend some time with their baby. The baby's name and measurements can be recorded, photographs can be taken, handprints and footprints made and a lock of the baby's hair collected. Some parents do find the contact with their baby comforting; others in their grief and in trying to cope may find this difficult.

You may wonder if you can be called a parent or recognised as such after the early loss of your baby. Acknowledge that you are a parent, a parent who has suffered the death of your child. Talking openly about your baby will help you and others accept that you are indeed a parent.

Tracy and Keith's story

Tracy and Keith are a typical Australian couple with the dream of owning their own home and being able to provide for their family. Their loss has changed the way they look at how fragile life is and how precious children are.

Tracy and Keith suffered two losses; the first was a little boy, a stillborn. The second was their third child, a miscarriage at five weeks. This intimate story gives an insight into how a couple deals with the tragic and unexpected loss of their two children.

Tracy's first pregnancy was fantastic and progressed well. When Tracy's waters broke, she wasn't fazed at all until she saw blood in the amniotic fluid. After arriving at the hospital, she was asked if she could feel the baby kick, and she answered, 'Yes'. As a precaution she was sent to have an ultrasound and it was soon after that Tracy and Keith's worst fears were realised.

A second ultrasound confirmed there was no heartbeat and that our little boy Nathan had died. At that stage, they didn't know what had gone wrong. They later confirmed Nathan had died, because when the cord attached to the placenta, mine was attached by very thin fibres on the edge of the placenta . . . all the fluid gushing out when my waters broke pulled all the fibres away, so all the blood loss or what I thought was my blood loss was actually my son bleeding to death.

Tracy found that small rituals helped her feel that she was not alone.

There was a book in the parents' room [at the hospital], where parents would sign what they felt, or a note to their baby. I put my son's handprint in there and put a note next to the handprint. Although it's sad it helps to know you're not alone.

Not only was there the grief of the loss to deal with, but other emotions and thoughts came up, shaking Tracy's self-confidence.

I felt the first thing I could give Keith in our marriage turned out to be a failure, I failed him and I also felt that my body had failed my son.

Her third pregnancy ended at five weeks, and Tracy kept herself isolated from friends after this, finding that the death of two children was very difficult to cope with. She felt she was lucky to have the support of her and Keith's families to get them through this time. She knew she had people close to her who she could cry openly with and let out her grief.

We always had family members from both sides ringing or coming over to see us.

Dealing with the premature loss of a child is difficult for both parents and places a tremendous amount of pressure on any relationship, no matter how strong it is. As Keith acknowledges, *It wasn't easy for the first couple of years. We still have a birthday for him, have a cake and have people come over and sing happy birthday. We have his ashes in a little angel urn; it sits up on the mantelpiece. We still give him something for Christmas and put it in the stockings.*

Tracy and Keith have two other children, a daughter and a son, and have explained to them why there are two extra presents under the Christmas tree each year.

We always tell our two that are alive that that's from their brother and possibly a brother or sister . . .

It actually helps keep him and our miscarriage alive, in a funny sort of way. My daughter and I have even got halfway through a scrapbook of Nathan . . . My little one wants to look through it and tell everyone that's his big brother in heaven.

Dealing with the grief can be ongoing and can affect a family in many different ways for long periods of time. The loss of a little one is always there and is always part of the family's life history. Tracy and Keith feel that it is important that their children do see them remember and, at times, grieve for the children lost as it helps the surviving children understand what has happened in the family.

The hardest part about losing a baby early is that the death doesn't always seem real to friends and family.

Most of the time your family and friends haven't been through it. They can listen to you but they can't say, 'I know what you're talking about.' It's just that they don't know what to say, that's why. They know 'sorry' isn't enough.

Keith had a cousin and I noticed she was one of the only ones who didn't ring. I rang her and said to her, 'You don't know what to say do you?' She just cried. I said not to cry. She said, 'I don't know what to say to you that's why I didn't ring. Don't think I don't love you. Don't think I don't feel but there's no words.'

I said, 'Yes, I know, there are no words.'

Gavin and Kelly's story

Gavin and Kelly are an example of a couple who have
shared their pain and supported each other through
the difficult loss of their daughter, Alexandra, in April
2006. Gavin and Kelly also found that they grieved in
individual ways.

After having a healthy son Harry in 2005, Gavin and Kelly
quickly fell pregnant with their second child. The 12- and
20-week scans appeared normal, but Kelly's baby bump was
much bigger than it should have been for the scheduled
dates. Warning bells sounded and Gavin and Kelly went
through a series of tests – to discover that their second
baby had a lethal genetic disorder.

*At about 30 weeks, Kel was huge. She was more like 34 weeks.
We had all these tests trying to work out what the problem was.
At 32 weeks we were shattered with the news that our baby had
a genetic disorder that would ultimately take her life. There was
nothing that could be done other than to palliate our baby if she
was born alive. Alex had been such an active baby in the womb.
It seemed incomprehensible that the pregnancy was taking such
a devastating turn. Kelly was told by her doctor that she would
have to be induced due to threatening pre-eclampsia. We were sent
to the NICU [Neonatal Intensive Care Unit] to speak with a
paediatrician who explained what would happen to Alex if she was
born alive. Our dear little baby would not live for very long.*

*Despite the heartache of what was to come, we were comforted
by the compassion of the doctors who cared for and supported us.
The doctor who delivered the diagnosis was kind and beautiful to
us. There were so many things that made a difference in those days*

before delivering Alex. Most of all was the kind and compassionate care of those around us. I will never forget the doctor had tears in her eyes when telling us Alex had this condition.

Gavin and Kelly had a day to prepare for their baby's birth. *We found a beautiful little outfit for baby Alex to wear when she was born, and a special bunny rug for her which we had her big brother Harry sleep with the night before, so she could know what her brother smelt like. We prepared ourselves as much as we could for what lay ahead. Two of Kel's close friends came over to be with Kel.*

The morning of the induction arrived. We desperately wanted Alex to be born alive. She had survived this far, we wanted to hold her in our arms, alive, even for the briefest of times, and comfort her. Unfortunately the labour progressed very badly, and Kelly haemorrhaged. 'Code Pink' was called over the PA, and the room filled with doctors and nurses. The doctor turned to me and said, 'It's about Mum now.'

With those words Kelly and Gavin knew that their daughter had died. It was extremely difficult for Kelly, she had to continue to deliver the baby.

The other concern I had was, 'How am I going to do this? [It was really difficult to] get my head around what I had to do to get Alexandra out.

A couple of hours later I birthed our baby. The poor little darling had been so close to being born alive, it was shattering to have never felt her heartbeat. We spent the next 24 hours in hospital with our precious baby. Creating memories, and loving her. We took lots of photos, and had Harry come in to meet his sister. He was so young he won't remember it, but we wanted to be able to show him a photo of him with his sister when he is older.

The following day Gavin and Kelly had to leave their

baby. *The hardest moment was leaving Alexandra, actually separating themselves from her.*

How do you walk away? We moved to the lift lobby and were surrounded by pregnant women and people with babies. Happy people, visiting live babies. Kelly couldn't cope, we went into the stairwell, and commenced our journey home to grieve.

After going home, Gavin and Kelly found strength in each other. Gavin found dealing with the outside world very hard at first, particularly coping with his own grief, organising the funeral, and looking after Kelly and Harry.

I was the buffer between Kelly and the world. Kelly shut down emotionally after the birth. She didn't want to see or speak with anyone. She was in a very sad and dark place. When she was ready Kelly found comfort in our support network of special friends and professionals. This was crucial for Gavin's and Kelly's emotional recovery.

There were friends that amazed us with their efforts to comfort and support us.

Gavin and Kelly have created some mementoes to keep Alexandra's memory alive, to acknowledge her place in their family.

We have a beautiful photo of Alex's little feet, placed with the first photos of our other children. On her birthday we have a family dinner, and the boys send balloons up to Alex in heaven.

Gavin and Kelly found the subsequent pregnancy after Alex difficult. The anxiety and stress of being pregnant was intense, hoping that this time they would leave hospital with a healthy baby.

The innocence and the naivety of the pregnancy is gone for us. It's like we are half expecting this to go sour.

With deep joy and relief, Gavin and Kelly welcomed

Archie Alexander Michael safely into the world on 9
April 2007. Archie was due on the first anniversary of
Alex's stillbirth, and is the long-awaited baby brother for
Harry. Felix Alexander Troy, their third son, was born on
8 December 2008.

Isobel's story

Isobel was married in 1965 and longed to have a large
family, assuming that all would go to plan. She found that
falling pregnant was difficult and when she finally became
pregnant it was a bittersweet moment.

*I'd always wanted four or six children. My husband and I had
two children, Peter in 1967 and Kylie in 1968. At the age of
27, and trying for another baby unsuccessfully and having every
test possible back then, there were two years with my doctor
checking everything, being poked and probed to find the problem,
thermometer under the pillow, taking my temperature every morning until they finally tested my husband and found that he had
a low sperm count.*

Isobel was pregnant with twins and she was thrilled
with the news. However, she started putting on an extreme
amount of weight, causing her doctor some concern.

*I was putting on 2 to 3 pounds [roughly 1 kilogram] a day
and I was getting really huge. The outside of my tummy, which was
blown up to the full length of my extended arm, was bleeding on
the outside. It turned out the top baby's kidneys weren't working
and [the waste was] just recycling into my body. Back then, they
didn't know or didn't appear to know about it. I was in a lot of*

pain for the last few months and they had me on 21 tablets a day for the pain.

Isobel went into labour at 26 weeks. The delivery and subsequent death of her twins was difficult and Isobel found it hard to accept the deaths because of the way the birth and her recovery were dealt with.

The labour started in the toilet at home at 26 weeks and within minutes of getting to the hospital the first baby arrived. The second baby came out with a gush of water, which was all his fluid, which really surprised everyone. They then gave me the injection and I went into a twilight zone.

After the births I was taken back to the normal maternity ward to recover and that was that.

Back then, babies born so small and underdeveloped at 26 weeks did not survive. My babies lived for only 12 minutes. The hardest part was that in such cases funeral arrangements were automatically made. There was also a lack of caring and sensitivity in dealing with the emotional and physical trauma of having a stillbirth.

I never saw our twins. I can remember the nurse walking past me with one but everyone was so busy up the other end I didn't seem to matter. I really just wanted to hold them. I wanted to prove that I wasn't dreaming. I had to switch off to stop being hurt so much.

The twins' burial was at the Melbourne Cemetery. I was still in hospital, so they wouldn't let me go to the funeral. I wanted to go, but the cemetery people advised me not to because they hadn't completed the area and they were putting other babies in there. The nurse said to me the twins should just be put in the incinerator. That is a comment I can never forget. They gave me the bill for the funeral. It was more expensive to bury them than to have them. A letter from the government arrived asking which twin was born first, which was really difficult to accept or believe that they were asking me this.

The memory of her tiny twins remains with Isobel, even though she didn't see their little faces after their birth. Remembering them is still very difficult and always brings up the underlying emotional hurt at losing them. She also remembers very clearly the day that she left the hospital, her arms empty.

March is a different month. I live that day again. I see the nurse's face. Before I checked out of the hospital, my husband and I went and looked at the healthy new babies in the ward and thought about how lucky people were if only they realised. We walked out of the hospital, the door closed and that was it. You walk out with nothing.

Learning to go back to life before the pregnancy was hard. Isobel felt that it was as if she was never pregnant and her twins never existed. Having no strong support network also made coming to terms with the deaths and recovering from the hurt very difficult. She also experienced feelings of anger at people's lack of understanding and thoughtlessness.

No comment from anybody. My husband said, 'It was meant to be.' No support from either of our parents. Nobody knew what to say.

I put a birth notice in the paper and the Mormons turned up at my door a few days later, wanting to explain the meaning of life and the meaning of death. I'm not a very angry person, but with huge boobs and a lot of sadness in my heart I did slam the door in their face.

Isobel and her husband tried to deal with the tragedy in their own ways. It is something that they find difficult to talk about still.

My husband said to just get on with life but I didn't want to get on with it, we both hurt. He remembers, but it's a closed book. He is better with grandchildren than he was with his own as these days there is much more time and times have changed.

Despite being told not to have any more children, Isobel became pregnant again very quickly. She and her husband refused to give up. Her next two boys weren't replacements for the twins but did complete the family. These days, she is proud of her nine wonderful grandchildren.

Marie's story

Marie Field is the doting mother of Anthony Field, the blue Wiggle, and Paul Field, The Wiggles' manager. The Wiggles have been ambassadors of the Bonnie Babes Foundation for the past 13 years.

Marie has bravely decided to share her, until now, untold story. This is a story of a mother's hopes and dreams for her baby and how she faced the trauma of a stillbirth.

I was born in 1933, and I was 22 when I was married. When I became pregnant I was so proud and thrilled about it, and then, about seven months into the pregnancy, the movements stopped. I mentioned this to the doctor and he said that the baby [Mary] could be dead. Because of the lack of technology in those days, I had to carry the baby until the doctor could be certain that there was no sign of life. When this was ascertained, I had a long and difficult labour, and no precious baby to show for it.

It was a terrible time for my husband and I, we just turned to each other. We had an extraordinary, wonderful marriage, and it was a terrible shock. I kept thinking that this couldn't be happening to us — it will go away.

I used to play the piano back in those days, and I think music helped me through that, music helps me still.

My husband, John, suffered a terrible stroke, and 14 months later he had a fatal stroke. John was in a coma for eight days before he died, and our seven children all came in and stayed with him and me. We had soft music playing the whole time he was slipping away, and the children held their father's hands and sang to him. We somehow survived that awful time with the help of a wonderful priest, Father Paul Glynn, who brought us all a great deal of peace. I know that spirituality brought us all great comfort.

We always remember Mary at Christmas time and on her birthday every year. There was no counselling available to me after Mary died, but I found great peace in the counselling that I had after my husband died, it was really tremendous help in getting me through that dreadful, sad time. All the sadness still surfaces on birthdays and on special anniversaries.

Annie and Richard's story

Annie and Richard are a couple who have worked through Richard's grief after the death of his stillborn son with his first wife. Annie has helped Richard take positive steps towards acknowledging his son's death and setting up rituals and memories at Dean's burial site to help him with the guilt that has affected him for many years.

Richard had the responsibility of making the final decision to turn off his newborn son's life support. For many years, Richard has used drugs and alcohol to block out the guilt. In 1972, Richard's son Dean was almost stillborn. The cord was wrapped around his neck and he needed a respirator.

His wife was heavily sedated and Richard had to make the decision on his own. The doctor said the baby was brain dead, 'So turn it off'.

The decision meant guilt for many years. I only had closure when I found out where he was buried. It was 28 years later.

Richard struggled with drug and alcohol addiction. When Annie met him she managed to get him to open up as to what was contributing to his self-destructive behaviour. She realised that finding his baby would help Richard recover. Annie organised a plaque and they said their prayers, lit candles and set the plaque. Annie confidently outlines the emotional strength that Richard, and many people, needed to find to be able to face their grief.

It's coming to terms and then going forward, finding a positive outcome makes you a stronger person. The thing is, there's nothing for men. Nowhere for men to turn to. Richard had a high-pressure job in a merchant bank. They think men should be strong enough, but he hasn't got over it. The sympathy all goes to the mother [his ex-wife] and in those days a man showing tears was like a weak species. His boss said to him, 'Compassionate leave is only two days.'

Annie and Richard also describe how difficult it is for a man to openly show his grief, which tends to compound the problem.

The Australian way is to be macho and not show feelings, there's a fear their mates will look down on them. I've been able to get Richard to cry after bottling everything in. Crying shows you're compassionate, caring and loving.

Connie and George's story

With a family history of difficult pregnancies, Connie had
experienced two miscarriages before becoming pregnant
for the third time. Her own mother had a history of
difficult pregnancies, dying during childbirth when
pregnant with Laurence (Connie's brother); similarly,
Connie's pregnancy with John Peter was difficult.

*I'd had problems all along. About six weeks along I was crossing
the road, and there was a woman crossing the road with her kids,
and one of the kids jumped out of the pusher and ran onto the
road into traffic. It caused me a terrible shock. I started spotting,
and was put in hospital after my waters broke at seven months.
They wanted to make sure there was no infection.*

*After spending six weeks in hospital, just three days before his
due date, John Peter was stillborn on 22 February 1971.*

It was hard, there was no one to talk to in those days.

*My family were all living 30 miles [48 kilometres] away, I
had no close support.*

Connie was in hospital for two weeks following the
birth of John Peter. Her husband, George, came and saw
her in the hospital, and was able to see the baby before
John Peter was buried without a funeral.

*They said I was too weak to see the baby, so I never got to
see him or hold him. He was buried in Fawkner Cemetery in a
communal grave. They weren't going to tell us that originally — my
husband had to insist on finding out where he was buried.*

*They didn't allow you to put up plaques in those days, so
there's no way of knowing exactly where John Peter is.*

George was a wonderful support to Connie, but he had
to go to work to support his family.

We had two children, and it was hard, having to look after them, with one in the cot.

Neighbours helped, they were supportive which was good.

Ten minutes after I was home, the health nurse came to visit. They hadn't told her that he had been stillborn. That was difficult.

They had told me all along that I had no infection, but after the birth I had a doctor and some students come around a few days later, and I think they thought I couldn't understand English since I was an immigrant, but they said that had the baby survived he would have had brain damage from the infection in the uterus. That was a bit of comfort to me, that he wasn't brought into the world like that.

As her mother had died in childbirth, Connie was rather scared throughout the pregnancy, and believes that if there was more support on offer in those days then she certainly would've accepted it.

If I wasn't in this country I think I would've ended up like my mother, so that's something to be thankful for.

Connie and George have been married for almost 49 years now, and have three healthy grown-up sons, and six grandchildren.

Learning to cope with stillbirth and neonatal death

Experiencing a stillbirth or a neonatal death is a traumatic event and it is essential that the parents be allowed to grieve in their own time and in their own way. There are some things that can be done to help deal with the pain and suffering that comes with the sudden loss of your baby.

Involve your family and friends
- Call on your family and friends to help share your grief and to set up some support contacts and networks. Support is essential to help you move on with the grieving process. If friends and family ask if they can help, don't hesitate to give specific suggestions that you feel would make things easier, such as meals, company or childcare.

Look after your physical wellbeing
- You will feel emotionally tired and drained but it is important to make sure that you are eating well and managing to rest and exercise to help with your recovery. Staying healthy and rested will help overcome the emotional tiredness that you will feel as a response to your intense grief.

Talk or write about your baby and your feelings
- It sometimes helps to verbalise or write down the feelings that you are experiencing. Ignoring or trying to forget how you are feeling is not helpful to the grieving process. Write your feelings down in a journal. Make a baby book with mementoes, cards, keepsakes, etc, to help keep a memory of your baby.

Acknowledge your parenthood
- Remember that you are a parent and that you have had a child and have memories of that child. Don't be afraid to talk to others about the birth and death of your child, to help others realise that you are a parent.

Common Questions

We have been told that our baby is dead or will die. What do we do?

Dealing with this news is confronting and can be confusing. You may instinctively wonder how to respond and how to parent your child. It is always the parents' right to be with their baby as much as they want, to handle or hold them during their last minutes or hours. Always make your decisions based on the information given and by asking questions of your healthcare provider. There is also no need to hurry as decisions can change as parents work out what is right for their baby and themselves.

What practical arrangements need to be made?

A baby's birth and death needs to be registered at 20 weeks according to federal laws. Babies who are born from 20 weeks of pregnancy onwards receive a birth and death certificate, and cremation and burial arrangements can be made. Your healthcare provider will be able to help you with the formalities to register your details. Burial or cremation can either be organised by the hospital or the parents can make their own arrangements.

I still look pregnant. How will my body recover?

The physiological responses to giving birth will continue and, at times, be distressing. The mother's body will respond as it would after a normal birth. Hormonal changes following the delivery of the baby can cause mood swings. The mother's body will still look pregnant but over time, sometimes many months – will return to normal. It is a difficult period and it is important that the grieving mother is kind to herself and tries not to rush 'getting over the birth' too quickly.

Our baby passed away but I still have breast milk. How can I stop it?

It can be very distressing for women following the death of their baby as their body will still produce breast milk. This is one of the most difficult issues that grieving mothers have to cope with, both physically and emotionally. This can seem so unfair when their baby has died, yet their body continues to function as it would if the baby were alive.

Generally it takes several days for breast milk to dry up. To speed up this process, it is important to avoid touching your breasts, and to avoid expressing milk. (If you do this your breasts will keep on producing milk.) Medication can be used to stop milk production.

I can still feel my baby kick or cry at night. Why?

This is a very real phenomenon. Many mothers whose babies die in utero or very shortly after birth are quite certain they feel their baby kick, even days and weeks later. These feelings seem real. It is important to talk about what is going on with your body with a sensitive support person – family member, friend or counsellor – to understand that this is a normal reaction.

What is the risk of a stillbirth happening in a following pregnancy?

Parents who have had a stillbirth can often fear that this will happen again, although the risk is low for most couples. The risk of having a stillbirth may be higher if a chronic maternal health condition, such as diabetes, caused the previous problems. It is important to talk to your doctor or healthcare provider if there are concerns about going through another pregnancy.

Is there a length of time I should wait before having another baby?

The decision to try for another baby can be difficult. In some couples, the desire to have a baby immediately is strong in order to heal some of the pain of the previous loss. In other couples a waiting period is more suitable as they feel that they can become emotionally and physically strong enough to cope with the fluctuating emotions that will come with the following pregnancy.

Resources

Suggested reading:

Bonnie Babes Foundation, *You Are Part of Our Lives and Will Always Live in Our Hearts*

Peppers, L. and Knapp, R. *Motherhood and Mourning*, Praeger, New York, 1980

Schiff, H. *The Bereaved Parent*, Penguin Books, New York, 1978

For *My* *Little* *Peanut*

SAMANTHA SCHINNER

Where do I start? How do I feel? Sad, lonely, empty, cheated. Why my baby? You were my first little baby and I was so excited, so lucky to be having you. So what did I do wrong? Why did I have to lose you? For the best, they all said! How could losing my precious little peanut be for the best?
Time has moved on and the empty feelings have gradually subsided, the memory never fades and you will never be forgotten. So how do I feel now? I still think of you so often and feel that somehow you will always be near to me. Our time together was so precious and I am lucky to have experienced it. You will be forever tucked away in that special little place in my heart.
With all my love, your Mummy xxxx

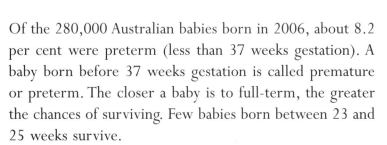

Chapter 6

Tiny miracles

Of the 280,000 Australian babies born in 2006, about 8.2 per cent were preterm (less than 37 weeks gestation). A baby born before 37 weeks gestation is called premature or preterm. The closer a baby is to full-term, the greater the chances of surviving. Few babies born between 23 and 25 weeks survive.

Delivering a very premature baby is a period of intense stress for the parents and family members. There is often a feeling of a loss of control and a feeling of helplessness as the parents are unable to 'protect' their baby as they had imagined. It is often very easy for disappointment to spill over into feelings of guilt. Some mothers of premature babies feel guilty that they didn't carry their baby to full-term, they didn't have a normal labour and aren't able to look after the baby after the birth. It is not your fault. Support from medical staff and friends and family is crucial during this time.

It is common for parents to feel a range of emotions, including fear, worry, confusion, vulnerability and grief.

Premature babies

Few parents have any warning that their baby is going to arrive prematurely. But whether you have known for a few weeks, a few days or just a few hours, the first day is full of anxiety and shock. Getting used to the environment of the Special Care Baby Unit (SCBU) or Neonatal Intensive Care Unit (NICU) in which your baby will be cared for is difficult as your baby will be surrounded by a great deal of hi-tech equipment, with sensors attached to every available space on your baby's body, and the busyness of the healthcare staff working in the units.

If your baby has been born prematurely, doctors will assess your baby's health to check heartbeat, breathing, level of activity, and colour that indicates how much oxygen is in your baby's bloodstream. Your baby will appear very small and frail, and as there is little body fat your baby's skin will seem transparent. To keep your baby warm he or she will be placed in an incubator and will be monitored by a number of sensors. Your baby may also be attached to a ventilator to help them breathe. Sometimes it will even be difficult to see your baby's face properly as they will be hidden behind a mass of tubes, wires and sticking plaster.

Your first visit will be daunting but nursing staff will do their best to make you feel welcome. You will be introduced to the nurse looking after your baby and they will give you some brief instructions on how to keep in contact with your baby. You may stay with your baby in intensive care as long as you like.

Doctors need to assess your baby's health as soon as possible to pinpoint any problems. One of the first things they will do is insert a fine tube into one of your baby's veins, either in the hand, foot, scalp or umbilical cord. This tube will be attached to a drip that sends nutrients into your baby's bloodstream. An additional tube may be placed in an artery, sometimes via the umbilical cord, so that doctors can take blood samples that will be taken every few hours to check the level of oxygen in the blood. Various intravenous lines, fluids and medicines will be attached to your baby's umbilical cord. This does not hurt your baby.

Love in a humidicrib

Being with your baby as much as possible is an essential part of the care of your baby. Learning when your baby is stressed and needs to rest and when your baby is ready to bond with you is one of the most important things you can do. This will also help you interact with your baby and get a sense of what your baby likes, such as hand holding, talking, singing or head stroking, which will help you and your baby to establish a bond.

Nurses in a neonatal unit will always be able to give you advice as it may be daunting at first to touch your tiny, fragile baby. But touching, handling and cuddling your premature baby is very important for both you and the baby and this will be positively encouraged.

It is understandable that some parents feel that their baby will bond with the doctors and nurses who are caring for him or her. But your baby needs you for love and support. To let your baby know that you are close by, try some of the following:

- Talk to your baby. Your baby can hear your voice even if some of the medications given prevent a response.

- Sit with your partner on either side of your baby and talk to each other. Talk about anything you can think of in quiet, calm voices so that your baby becomes accustomed to hearing you. Remember, your voices are already familiar and soothing. Reach out and touch your baby. As your baby grows there will be different ways to touch them.

As your baby's health improves, it's often possible to be allowed to place your baby on your lap – or you may be allowed to place the baby skin-to-skin on your chest under your shirt or a warm blanket or to give the baby kangaroo care.

Understanding the science

A baby born at full-term will have taken 38 to 40 weeks to mature and develop into a healthy being. If your baby is born early, the body and organs, especially the lungs, won't be as well developed as they should be and, as a result, your baby may have some serious health problems to overcome, including breathing problems, keeping warm and feeding.

Common complications of a premature baby include:

- Lung disease – premature babies often require oxygen via a ventilator or an incubator until their lungs are fully matured.
- Feeding difficulties – premature babies are often unable to suck and require a tube into the stomach until the sucking and swallowing reflex is developed.
- Temperature control difficulties – the control centre in premature babies' brains is immature and this is why babies are often cared for under special overhead heaters

or in enclosed incubators until they are mature enough to be cared for in a normal cot.

- Apnoea – this is when breathing stops for a short period of time. Breathing is controlled by a part of the brain called the respiratory centre, which often doesn't function properly in premature babies.
- Bradycardia – a slowing down of the heart rate, usually caused by apnoea.
- Jaundice – the baby's skin takes on a yellow colour, due to a compound in the blood called bilirubin, which breaks down red blood cells. A premature baby's liver is too immature to process the bilirubin properly, so phototherapy lights are used.

There could be many other treatments related to your baby's care and they depend on the type of complications or developmental care that your baby needs. The important thing to remember during the time your baby is in intensive care is to raise any questions that you may have with your medical team and hospital staff so that you are informed of what is being done for and to your baby. Lullabies and music played to premature babies have been shown to be comforting to them. When your premature baby is taken home, learning infant massage can assist your premmie baby to adjust to this type of contact and help with the bonding process. For more information on baby bonding and infant massage go to www.pinky-mychild.com.

Jillian and Jonathon's story

Jillian and Jonathon are both realists and it took great
courage for them to tell their story.

At 25 weeks, Jillian went for a check-up with her doctor
and he admitted her to hospital because her baby son was
smaller than he should have been. Once in hospital Jillian
found it difficult to believe what was happening to her and
her concern for her baby was overwhelming.

*I spent two weeks in hospital, ultrasounds daily, CTGs daily
[to check the baby's heartbeat] and bed rest . . .*

*We got to 26 weeks and then we made it to 27 and Oliver
was delivered. His breathing was pretty good, although he was on
a ventilator for 12 hours.*

Jillian and Jonathon discovered how unpredictable the
development and stabilisation of a premature baby can
be. The first week seemed okay but the following weeks
became extremely stressful. It was during this time that
Jillian and Jonathon took comfort from the help and the
care of the nurses in the neonatal intensive care unit.

*All of a sudden Oliver started having trouble feeding – I
couldn't feed him properly and then he ended up on breathing
support.*

*I felt close to the nurses. We were told to stay away at one stage,
because they were concerned about our health.*

*The sisters around you are keeping such a close eye on other
problems, equipment like ventilators, you're just waiting for
something more serious to happen. They are easy to understand
and empathic people.*

Jillian and Jonathon found it therapeutic and helpful

to set up a website to track the progress of Oliver and to allow family and friends to follow his progress rather than Jillian and Jonathon having to relay the same information over and over again to different people.

I wanted to know whether he was going to survive or not – just to get the day by day, not wanting to talk about it again and again. What we did was set up a website for Oliver, so that people could log in and have a look at how he is progressing.

The social worker had actually told me to set it up and I thought it was just great that other people could look at it. I just downloaded the photos at work and uploaded them onto the site. I could update milestones, and we had a book that people could write in. Like when he cracked the 1kg mark, as he was only 775 grams when he was born . . .

Jillian and Jonathon found that mostly people were supportive and in their busy lives, working and then seeing Oliver at the hospital, Jillian did get comfort from other mothers in the neonatal intensive care unit.

Jonathon and I would see Oliver in the morning and then would head off to work, and then we'd come back afterwards and stay there until late. I would usually be there with Oliver for at least 12 hours a day. Other mums, they'd come along and have a look at Oliver and ask what was going on with him and it was nice to have someone ask.

You do meet people in the unit with much worse problems but you really get caught up with what is going on with your baby and your own life.

Helen's story

Helen is a businesswoman who combines her professional
work with her role as a mother.

Early on in her pregnancy, Helen started putting on weight
and at 30 weeks she was diagnosed with pre-eclampsia. The
doctor broke Helen's waters and she had an emergency
caesarean. Her baby, Tarryn, became distressed and was
taken to a neonatal intensive care unit.

*I didn't see her for two days, that was heartbreaking. Having an
emergency, they knock you out completely and everyone sees your
baby before you do. She was only about 3 pounds 8 [1.7 kilograms]
when she was born, so she was quite little and we couldn't touch
her or hold her.*

*It was pretty heartbreaking having her in there, she had to
stay for three weeks. Dad would take me in every day so I could
feed her myself — in the night-time they would feed her. I stayed
in hospital for 10 days and I had the best of care.*

With the premature birth of baby Tarryn, Helen kept
asking herself why her baby was born so early. As with many
parents of premature babies there is the feeling of guilt that
something was done that caused the early birth.

*You have this guilt. What did I do? Did I eat something? Did
I eat all the bad foods? I was smoking as well. That's why she was
born so early. So you go through all those guilty emotions.*

*But I think with women, you become very emotional. Guilt.
Why are you being punished? People who go to full-term and
have stillborns, does the guilt feel different?*

Rose and Jim's story

Rose and Jim are the proud parents of Millie and Sophie,
ten-year-old charmers who have been in Bonnie Babes
Foundation publicity and awareness campaigns because
they had been born so very prematurely and the Bonnie
Babes Foundation raised funds for vital medical equipment
which helped the twins' survive. Theirs is an important
story to tell.

Rose and Jim experienced a number of miscarriages and a
33-week stillbirth. They had reached a stage in their lives
where they felt they would never recover from the grief
of their lost babies and almost came to the decision not to
continue to try having children because of the heartache
they had experienced. Then they fell pregnant with twins.
Rose went into labour early in her pregnancy but her
doctor was able to stop it. She was admitted to hospital
and had to stay in bed.

*It was ten days before they were born. Everyone seemed quite
comfortable that I'd be able to hang on.*

*Then it all just went wrong again. I had a labour that they
managed to stop and then two days later, I was feeling really unwell
and uncomfortable. I called the nurse and told her that something
was wrong. She was quick to say that if there's an infection, you
probably have to deliver today. I'm like, 'I'm not going to listen
to you, you don't know anything, I'm going to wait.'*

Despite Rose's determination to hang on, she was rushed
up to an emergency delivery room where her doctor calmly
told her that the twins would only have a 40 per cent
chance of being born alive as they were only 23 weeks.

We thought that was reasonable odds, but that's for single babies. The doctor said, 'There's no guarantee about the quality of life, and you might want to think about, you know, what that means if they're very badly damaged.'

He also said, 'If they come out punching and looking like they really want to live, we'll resuscitate them; but if they come out looking very weak, it's up to you, but we prefer not to resuscitate them?'

I said, 'Well, yeah, that sounds reasonable.'

The twins were born and then rushed to another room to be checked on by the medical staff. Rose suffered birth complications and both Jim and Rose were relying on the medical staff to keep them informed. When they finally did see their girls, Millie and Sophie, they fell in love with the tiny little babies.

I can remember looking at them that night and thinking, They're beautiful, they're just perfect, little, tiny babies. Looking at the photographs of them now; Oh my God, they're like sparrows.

Jim and Rose were thrown into shock seeing their girls in the neonatal intensive care unit, and had to learn to deal with feelings of not being in control of their daughters' care and wellbeing. They also had to learn how to hold and touch their babies and feed them by holding the intravenous tube. Jim fell instantly in love with Sophie and Millie but Rose found that it took her a while to bond because of the environment they were in and the fragility of the premature babies.

Most people like to have some control over their environment and outcomes, and when you realise you have no control . . . you've got to think about what happens either way.

I was scared they were going to die. It wasn't till I saw things being done to them that I started to bond. Then, all of a sudden, they were people that needed to be protected. I kept saying to the nurses there, 'If you're worried or if you think there's something wrong, you'll come and get me, won't you?'

And the babies were so sick, anything could go wrong. I remember one day they couldn't find a vein on their wrists or their ankles, and they tried their heads — they needed them for the antibiotics and fluids that kept them alive. So they had to get a surgeon over from the hospital who used a line into their groin so they could get to the heart.

Against the odds, little Sophie and Millie survived and are Rose and Jim's miracle babies. They are happy, healthy and energetic children who have just celebrated their tenth birthday.

They're very bright. And they're extremely supportive of each other and extremely competitive with each other at the same time. They make me laugh. They're just delightful.

I feel we're very lucky.

Steve and Janine's story

Steve and Janine are a brave and inspiring couple. Their baby, Matthew, was born at 24 weeks and survived, and the journey from his birth to the day he left hospital was long and intense.

The pregnancy was normal and all the scans didn't indicate any complications. When they returned from holidays, Janine felt intense pain but her labour was held off for a week, until her waters broke early. Their long journey had begun.

We hadn't had any experience with premature babies. You go

*through a broad range of emotions and you feel optimistic and
then you feel completely, totally scared. Janine was doing what
she had to do. One afternoon, a doctor came in to the room and
told us the potential outcome and risks [of having a baby at 24
weeks] and that we had to make a decision to resuscitate the baby,
if he wasn't breathing at delivery.*

*They thought there was very, very little chance of him breathing
on his own at birth and it was up to us to decide whether we
wanted the doctors to intervene.* Steve and Janine decided
that they wanted to do everything that they could to keep
Matthew alive. Baby Matthew came out breathing and Steve
and Janine didn't have to face the hard decision.

*He was only 720 grams and he actually came out, and cried.
They just put him on the bed for a few seconds and then took
him out to hook him up in intensive care. We didn't see him for
an hour and a half after that.*

As the time ticked on, Janine and Steve waited to hear
how he was going. When they were finally allowed to see
him, he was hooked up to the machines in the neonatal
intensive care unit. Rather than shock, both Janine and
Steve felt instant love.

*It was exciting to be able to go down to see him during the
day . . . He's your new son, but I was worried about our families,
because it's obviously a bit confronting. Everyone put on a brave
face, but everyone was a bit taken aback.*

*One of the consultants said, 'If you get through the first 72 hours,
I'll be very happy, if you get through the first week I'll be extremely
happy, and if he gets through the first month I'll be over the moon . . .'
So we were thinking in those sorts of increments of time.*

During the time Matthew was in intensive care, he would
be doing well and then take a big step backwards. Because

of his fragility it took both Steve and Janine a long time to be able to want to touch him as they were frightened of something going wrong.

Their older son, Toby, was three at the time and he adjusted very well to his parents spending most of their time at the hospital. To Toby, Matthew was still his little brother.

He handled it really well. I think that the hardest thing for him was us not being around that much but in terms of actually being in the hospital and seeing Matthew, it didn't faze him . . . I think he just thought that it was all pretty normal.

I think that once Matthew was born, and I got to sleep at home again, it was nice for him to have me back a little bit. We went in [to the hospital] every single day . . .

Steve and Janine made sure they were informed about every procedure undertaken or medication that was administered to Matthew so that they could understand what was being done.

We did a lot of research and every time one of the doctors would mention a drug or a procedure, we would look it up and it helped us. The consultant always said to us, 'We'll guide you and tell you the best things to do, but at the end of the day, you're his parents and you need to have input into what we do'.

Matthew was in hospital for 148 days and during that time his condition would change from good to bad from moment to moment, making the journey an emotional rollercoaster for his parents. They were always aware that he could be taken from them at any time and any time spent with him was precious. Matthew had chronic lung disease, a third of his bowel removed, continual problems with his lungs, concerns about the oxygen levels on the development of his eyes and his organs, 12 blood transfusions; the list of treatment and setbacks was endless and very confronting.

The amazing thing with these prem babies is that things can change so suddenly. On one occasion it was literally within a space of 20 minutes. I think we'd just done his feeding and then we walked out of the room to get a sandwich and then came back and got pulled aside by one of the neonatologists who told me there'd been a change for the worse.

We'd call every night before we went to bed to find out how he was going and that was always nerve-racking because even though you only just left the hospital maybe an hour or so before, you were always frightened of what you were going to hear. Every day there was always something happening and I think that the experience of it all didn't really kind of hit us until sometime after we got him home.

Matthew began to make good progress at around 100 days and weighed in at 2.2 kilos. His parents were also encouraged to take him out of the humidicrib and cuddle him every day to help with his recovery and progress.

When he finally came home, after five months, Matthew began to smile. A personality trait that still continues to this day. He's now a cheeky boy who has a bubbly personality. Getting to his 12-month milestone was a joy for Steve and Janine.

I guess just getting to 12 months is a huge milestone for us. We're looking forward to less doctors appointments, seeing him grow and develop more. You know, we still find it amazing that he's so happy all the time with all he's been through. As soon as you walk in the room his face just lights up, he wants to be cuddled and be picked up.

He is quite ticklish, he likes to laugh. He is a very calm baby and is very content to just lie in his bed and play with his toys.

Faye's story

Faye Browne is the managing director for a fashion company. She is busy running her business while squeezing in looking after a growing family.

Faye's middle child was five or six weeks premature. At the time she already had a two-year-old baby. Life was hectic and looking back she doesn't know how she managed to find the time to juggle the care needed by her newborn, her young child and working.

My husband took the early shift at night and I'd take the shift after midnight because my son needed feeding every half hour. Life can't stop, you still have to clean the house, cook, look after the other child. I was part of the problem because I thought I could do it all and didn't take time off.

Learning to cope with having a premature baby

The most important thing to help through the birth and care of a premature baby is to make sure you are well-informed and have a strong support network, such as family, friends, a healthcare provider, support groups and other parents of premature babies. After the initial shock of experiencing the neonatal intensive care unit, the focus will be on your child and developing a bond with him or her to help with the recovery process.

Stay strong and positive
- Acknowledging and accepting your feelings about a premature birth is the first step toward coping. Either write down a list or talk to a friend or counsellor to help you identify how you are really feeling. Writing down

your emotions and experiences during the time your baby is in intensive care can be helpful in letting you know how far you have come with your baby's progress.

Remember that your baby needs you

- Be a parent to your baby. Spend time with your baby as often as you can. As soon as your baby is ready, ask the staff how you can assist. This will help you become more confident with your baby and get to know the signs that your baby is stressed or responding to you.

Make sure you ask questions and understand the medical procedures being done to your baby

- Ask questions, do research and become informed about what is being done in the care of your baby. The neonatal intensive care unit can be overwhelming and busy but if you understand some of the treatments or the reasons why certain procedures are being done you will eliminate some of the stress from feeling out of control and not being able to care for your baby completely.

Always check any concerns you have about your baby with your doctor or paediatrician

- All babies need a lot of care – but it is true that premature babies will require specialised care and there may be more challenges to face. Try not to worry, and be patient. Don't get disheartened if your baby has not reached a milestone which their peers have crossed – remember premature babies may have different growth patterns. Always mention your baby's due date and birth date to the doctor when you take them for a check-up.

Common Questions

Is our baby uncomfortable?

Some medical procedures, such as placing tubes in your baby, may cause slight distress and painkillers may be given. Once they are in place staff will ensure your baby is as comfortable as possible. If the baby shows signs of distress and tries to move a lot then your baby may be gently sedated or given painkillers.

Why can't I hold my baby?

Over the first few days or even weeks, your baby may be too fragile for you to cuddle – but it will make it even more special when you finally get to hold your baby for the first time. If your baby is well enough, you may be able to cradle their head in your hand. Once your baby is stable, you may be able to hold and cuddle the baby even if they are attached to a ventilator. In the meantime, you may be able to touch or gently stroke your baby.

Is there anything we can bring in for our baby?

At first your baby will probably be dressed only in a nappy so that staff can observe their condition and temperature more easily. It also means that there's less reason to handle the baby. When your baby is well enough, however, you may like to buy your baby an outfit – you can buy special premature-sized stretch-suits. Bonnie Babes has a special range in department stores for early arrivals, and the Bonnie Babes volunteers also knit and sew special premmie clothes given to families free of charge. You may also like to personalise your baby's incubator with a couple of small toys that don't obstruct the equipment. Older brothers and sisters might like to draw some pictures to decorate the incubator or you could attach a family photograph.

We feel so helpless. Is this normal?

There is very little on a practical level that parents can do in the early days. However, if you planned to breastfeed, you can help your baby by expressing breast milk. Your midwife will give you all the help you need.

As soon as your baby is well enough for you to join in providing care, the nurses will be only too pleased to show you other ways in which you can be involved. It's easy to feel that there's nothing you can do for your baby. Simply being there benefits your baby. Even if your baby is sedated, they will still be able to tell if you're there by the sound of your voice and the feel of your touch. If your baby is well enough, you may be able to change the nappy though you're bound to feel nervous at first. This will get easier as time passes. It will help you to get to know your baby and help you build up confidence when handling them.

I feel awkward asking questions. Is this normal?

There will be so much going on around you that it will be impossible to take it all in at once. The staff will understand what a difficult time it is for you and will be happy to answer your questions, even if you have to ask more than once.

Write down any questions you have so that you don't forget them. You may also find it helpful to jot down the answers so that you can go over them in your own time.

What if our baby dies?

Although all parents worry about their baby dying, many babies in special care do survive and grow up to become healthy children and adults.

Even if your baby is very ill, try not to worry that you're getting 'too involved'. It's perfectly normal to become attached to your baby and it may help you cope later if your baby does sadly die.

It can take a very long time to come to terms with the loss of your baby. Your baby may have only had a short life but even if you tried to distance yourself you will have become involved emotionally.

The hospital will help you make necessary arrangements if this happens to you. It is also your choice as to what you want to do to remember your baby – holding and cuddling, washing and dressing, taking photographs. The medical staff can also put you in contact with a counsellor or a suitable support group.

Resources

Miracle Babies

Miracle Babies honours and celebrates the birth of babies who enter our world challenged by prematurity or sickness.

Melinda Cruz
Miracle Babies
PO Box 95
Moorbank
NSW 1875
Phone: 1300 PREMMIE (1300 773 664)
Email: info@miraclebabies.com.au

Preterm Infants' Parents' Association Inc. (PIPA)

The Preterm Infants' Parents' Association was formed in Brisbane in 1980 with the goal of offering support to the families of premature babies born in Queensland. The primary aim of the Association is to provide practical and emotional support to the parents and families.

PO Box 400
RBH, QLD 4029
Phone: (07) 3216 5114
www.pipa.org.au

The Bonnie Babes Foundation provides asssistance for families with prematurely born babies with our qualified counsellors and we raise vital funds for medical equipment for neonatal areas within hospitals.

Chapter 7

What to do when things aren't right

In current antenatal practice, many women are scheduled for regular check-ups and scans at regular intervals to keep track of where their pregnancy is up to and the health of the baby and mother. If anything of concern does come up in a check-up or scan, the healthcare provider will investigate and consult with the parents as to what can be done to minimise any threats to the baby's or mother's health or to make them aware of any possibility of complications through pregnancy. If something does not 'feel right' during your pregnancy it is important that you raise any concerns you may have with your healthcare provider as soon as possible.

Pregnancy complications for mother and baby

Some of the most common complications include the following:

Incompetent cervix

This condition is when the cervix opens before the baby is full-term. It means that the cervix opens without labour starting and can lead to miscarriage or a premature birth. It is a condition that will often happen again in other pregnancies. Treatment involves bed rest and reduced physical activity or involves a doctor putting a stitch in the cervix to keep it from opening too early. The stitch is removed when it is time for the baby to be delivered.

Gestational diabetes

This type of diabetes develops during pregnancy. About five per cent of pregnant women in Australia develop GDM. If gestational diabetes is left untreated, the baby risks becoming too large (increasing the risks of a vaginal delivery) or dying in the newborn period. Pregnant women are screened, via blood tests, for gestational diabetes. Treatment involves controlling it with diet and exercise or insulin injections and the monitoring of blood sugar levels.

Pre-eclampsia / High blood pressure

Pre-eclampsia is the most serious medical disorder of pregnancy and involves very high blood pressure, the appearance of protein in the urine and generalised swelling of body tissues, although not all women have all these symptoms. When pre-eclampsia affects the placenta, the baby's health and growth could be compromised. Pre-eclampsia only occurs during pregnancy, usually in the second half. The only known treatment for severe pre-eclampsia usually involves the delivery of a baby prematurely for the sake of the mother's health. Pre-eclampsia is not felt by the mother in the early stages of the disease but can be screened for through regular blood pressure checks and urine testing.

Preterm labour
Preterm labour is labour that occurs before the thirty-
eighth week of pregnancy and can happen to any pregnant
woman. Three groups of women are at greatest risk of
preterm labour and birth – women who have had a previous
preterm birth, women who are pregnant with twins or
multiple babies and women with certain uterine or cervical
abnormalities. Preterm labour may sometimes be stopped
with a combination of medication and rest. Ideally, birth
is delayed just long enough to transport the woman to a
hospital with a neonatal intensive care unit. Treatment with
a form of the hormone progesterone may help prevent
premature birth in some women who have already had a
premature baby.

Infections
Some infections, such as chickenpox, fifth disease, listeriosis,
rubella, salmonella and toxoplasmosis have the potential to
cause complications during pregnancy. As part of a pregnant
woman's check-up, your healthcare provider should be
informed of any illness that may not seem quite right or
does not clear up quickly.

Placental abruption
Placental abruption is a serious condition in which the
placenta separates from the wall of the uterus, partially or
completely, before delivery. If this happens, the baby can
be deprived of oxygen and nutrients and the mother can
experience life-threatening bleeding. Placental abruption
occurs in about one in 100 pregnancies. It happens most
often in the third trimester, but it can happen at any time

after the twentieth week of pregnancy. The main sign of placental abruption is bleeding. The baby may be delivered prematurely.

Placenta praevia
Placenta praevia is when the placenta implants very low in the uterus, covering all or part of the opening of the cervix. Placenta praevia occurs in about 1 in 200 pregnancies. In most women this is diagnosed in routine ultrasound scans. Placenta praevia diagnosed in the second trimester will sometimes correct itself; if not, the woman may have to stay in hospital towards the end of the pregnancy. A caesarean delivery is recommended for all women with placenta praevia as severe bleeding can occur if the baby passes through the placenta on delivery.

Janine's story

Janine is in her fifties and has suffered heartache. She has had two miscarriages and gave birth to a son at 26 weeks, who passed away six days later; this is a memory that she still carries with her.

I became pregnant quite easily and was grateful for that fact. Since my older sister was having fertility problems, I never took pregnancy for granted. The first miscarriage was hard enough, but the second one was devastating as I thought, Something is happening here . . . *a pattern was emerging.*

I was 36 and time was running out, so I couldn't afford to have another miscarriage. I again became pregnant quite easily. I was ecstatic and in hospital, the next day, I had a positive ultrasound.

*All was well. At 16 weeks, I had an amniocentesis, my choice.
I needed to be assured that the baby and the pregnancy were
going smoothly. I was hugely relieved that everything appeared
to be going very well. With every extra day, I became a little more
confident and, of course, feeling the baby kicking made every
minute very sacred to me.*

At 26 weeks, Janine suddenly experienced some potentially problematic symptoms and so was put back into
hospital for bed rest. Despite reassurances from the foetal
heart monitor and her obstetrician, not long after being
admitted to hospital she started haemorrhaging, forcing
the baby to be delivered immediately. Janine's only choice
was between an emergency caesarean or natural delivery.
Her son was delivered alive by caesarean section and given
a 50/50 chance of survival. The next six days proved to
be an emotional rollercoaster for Janine and her husband,
Werner.

*It was absolutely unbearable to be in the ward with all the new
babies. I was even sharing a double room with a girl in the bed next
to me and her new son. That was excruciating for me, especially
because my son had been taken to an intensive care nursery in
another hospital. Finally they agreed to put me on another floor,
near the nurses' station. The only problem with that was that I'd
be lying there awake all night, hearing the phone ring, thinking
it was the nurse calling to tell me my son had died.*

*My son lived only six days. I knew, had he survived, there could
have been some risk of brain damage, blindness and other problems.
In spite of this I was begging him to survive, I didn't care how.
Perfect or not I would have given my life for his.*

*I didn't give up hope right up until his condition finally
deteriorated to such a point that they assured us there was no*

chance of survival. Only then did we agree to shut down the support systems. Regardless of the assurances from the medical staff I was still so afraid that they would turn it off whilst there was still some hope.

He was clearly suffering and that was the most agonising aspect of the six days. Some people tried to tell us that he wasn't suffering but a mother knows. To this day, when I go back over his album the most difficult photos for me to look at are those on his last day before he died. He will always be in my heart, a part of who I am, and I will never stop grieving for him.

One of the most agonising aspects was that I was not allowed to pick him up and hold him until after he had died. All I could do was hold his little hand, dripping tears all over his face, as I whispered in his ears. It was an enormous relief just to hold him, even though he was dead. And I knew he was no longer suffering.

Janine will always treasure the memory of her little boy, who she named Joseph after her father's family, and not a day goes by without her thinking about him and what he would be doing if he had lived, a natural response to the loss of a child at such an early stage. To this day she feels like a mother without a child.

The night Joseph died I felt I could have held him to my chest forever . . . it was excruciating to let him go and allow them to take his body away. Coming home without him was also agonising. I had gone to the hospital with Joseph safely in my womb. I came home without him. The hard facts were that I had been pregnant and had delivered a son, who had lived and then died.

I decided to have some counselling a year later when a close friend became pregnant. I knew her pregnancy was going to be challenging for me. Joining a support group was also helpful for a short time. Then as other women found solace in their other children and increasingly had successful subsequent pregnancies, I felt I was alone with my childlessness, without the 'happy ending'. Later as I struggled unsuccessfully to conceive again I knew I didn't belong to the infertility group to which I had then turned for support. I knew what it was like to have a child and then to lose him. With these women I shared the longing, but they didn't know the feeling of being a mother without a child. Ultimately I didn't feel as though I belonged anywhere.

Time certainly helps but on occasions the pain is as raw as if I had lost Joseph yesterday. Sometimes, although not always, there are triggers such as when I was taking my sister's son to a school swimming group and sitting beside the pool with all the mums. As I was watching the children swimming, it was like this huge bolt of lightning hit me. I realised that Joseph would never swim. Of course, I knew intellectually that he would never swim, but it was like I had at that moment realised this for the first time. The magnitude of my loss was overwhelming. He will never have the experience of swimming with other kids and I will never sit by the pool with the other mums, watching him.

As they lowered his coffin into the ground, although numb, I remember feeling that I wished I could be buried with him. But, I had a choice. I believe we all have a choice with what we do in the wake of tragedy. My choice was to go on and embrace life fully as the new me. I will never be the person I was before Joseph lived and died, but I can be the new me with that loss incorporated as part of my very being. As I have sometimes expressed in my writing I often feel like I need to live life as fully as possible, not only for myself, but also for all my babies who were denied that opportunity, to do otherwise would be to compound the tragedy.

As I reflect on my life, the ache is always present. My babies *have helped me to come to terms with the knowledge that life is suffering and we must value every moment we have. As agonising as it is to look at Joseph's photos and to visit his grave, it remains a bittersweet experience. I am appreciative that I have those memories. It will always break my heart, but Joseph was loved a lifetime in his short six days.*

Julia's story

Julia's story deals with a spontaneous labour occurring at 24 weeks.

Julia's ordeal began with her 24-week check-up. She felt something was wrong, told her doctor and was put on steroids and other medications to stop early labour. Everything possible was done to stop Julia's labour but her baby was determined to be born. After 54 hours of labouring, Julia gave birth to a little girl, Stefani.

There was an 80 per cent chance that she was going to die, and basically they were all preparing me for the worst. But the midwives were absolutely wonderful. All you think about is, God! Let her live.

Julia and her partner, Felix, felt that they were instantly in sync with their tiny daughter. The process of waiting for their daughter to either survive or not was nerve-racking and painful.

What was amazing, though, is that Stefani was going in for her operation at only six weeks and weighing about 800 grams. Felix and I were in the parent room waiting for the doctor and the operation [wasn't due to] start until a few hours later. We were sitting in the room having a coffee, just holding each other's hands and praying and at one point in time I felt weird and my husband started having huge chest pains and I started feeling like I was about to pass out. I learnt later that that was the actual time that they started the operation, so I think that we must have some sort of connection.

I went and got some crystals and put them all in these good places to help her blood and help her breathing and to let her know that she was loved.

I think we pushed everybody away at that time who were supposed to be sharing our problems with us or our pain, but we weren't ready. I was so scared, one day she was alive, she was breathing, the next day she'd take two steps back.

When she was in hospital on the ventilator, with all this monitoring equipment attached to her, the nursing staff were really encouraging and pushed me to hold her, but I was scared. I would put my hand on her and I would hold my hand on her head and I would just talk to her. I just wanted her to know she was loved.

After Stefani came home I counted days, weeks, to make sure she was okay. In about six weeks I started to relax a little bit. I thought, My baby is home, she's alive so I must be doing everything right. She's still breathing. *Everything was getting better.*

Julia's story has a happy ending. After many weeks spent in intensive care, Stefani was allowed to come home. She is now six years old and has no developmental or health issues.

Maree's story

Maree Davenport (formerly Maree Luckins) MLC was elected
to represent Waverley Province in the Victorian Parliament's
Legislative Council in March 1996 at the age of 28; she'd
only been unsuccessful in the 1992 election by a mere 19
votes, when just 23. Not only was Maree the youngest woman
ever elected to the Victorian Parliament, she is also the first
Member of the Upper House to have had a baby while serving.
From 1996 to 1999, Maree served on the Joint All-Party
Scrutiny of Acts and Legislation Committee, as well as
many government policy committees in areas including the
Attorney-General, Fair Trading and Women's Affairs, Youth
and Community Services, Housing, Health and Aged Care,
Small Business and Industry, Science and Technology. From
1999, she was also Liberal Parliamentary Secretary for
Human Services. She lost her seat in the 2002 landslide.
Maree is married to Marcus Davenport and she has
three children.

Maree comes from a large family so she naturally assumed
that falling pregnant and carrying a baby to full-term was
the most natural and easiest thing to do. Her mother, Terri,
had had six kids in five years, including twins.

Having a miscarriage was a shock to Maree as her
mother was 'as fertile as a Mallee bull'. Maree had fallen
pregnant easily but lost this first baby. She sought support
to understand the reasons for her miscarriage but had
difficulty finding an organisation that offered any services
specific to pregnancy loss. Finally she heard about Bonnie
Babes and came into contact with people who made her feel
they understood her grief, and more importantly answered
her questions about miscarriage and what to expect.

Mum was as always a wonderful support, but she'd obviously had her crosses to bear as well. As we do in our family, you just move on. 'Okay darling, you've accepted that experience, grown from it, greater things will happen . . .'

Maree fell pregnant again but again had complications during her pregnancy.

In November 1994, I gave birth to my son, Cameron. I lost his twin during the pregnancy, which was confronting. The prospect of another loss was always at the back of my mind. I developed pre-eclampsia in the last trimester and by the time I was induced I was so swollen I looked like a blowfish! My blood pressure was dangerously high. In hospital I found myself attached to machines and confined to bed. My decision to have a drug-free birth was only made possible by the speed of his arrival — Cameron was posterior and broke my coccyx during birth. Sitting on a cushion for the next six months was worth it to have my beautiful big boy.

In 1996, when Cameron was 16 months, I was elected to Parliament and at the end of the year I fell pregnant with Brianna. While I worked as a Ministerial Advisor while pregnant with Cameron, the workload as an MP was extreme, coupled with having a young son. I'm always unwell when pregnant — all day sickness — so in Parliament I was very much trying to conceal my physical vulnerability because I was very conscious of maintaining a professional appearance. The Victorian, like all Australian Parliaments, was always a very male-dominated environment, with few women and scarcely any with dependent children. And, as sympathetic as blokes are to their own family, there is a competitive element there as well.

So at odd times during the pregnancy my 'condition' made me feel quite vulnerable. For example, a couple of times in the Chamber I took my shoes off under my desk because my feet were swollen. Once there was a snap division and I couldn't find my shoes. You can imagine the response from my parliamentary colleagues, yelling, 'Barefoot and pregnant'. I literally walked right into that one! So much for equality and the great strides made by the feminist movement.

I was extremely conscious that I was a trailblazer and I was determined that other women of childbearing age would not find it harder to seek and gain pre-selection because of the way I conducted myself while pregnant. Sadly, some people find dealing with women who are pregnant uncomfortable. There is even less understanding in the workplace for women suffering complications, let alone the loss of a much wanted baby.

My experiences made me decide to become more actively involved with the Bonnie Babes Foundation, so I could help other women and their families. The Foundation also does so much to help people who have premature babies.

Brianna was born unexpectedly and quite early as a result of pre-eclampsia again. The fetal monitor was showing she was increasingly distressed and I was quite panicky, with my blood pressure dangerously high. I was horrified to see the cord around her neck. She was completely blue and had to be resuscitated. Brianna [now twelve] is . . . the most beautiful, gorgeous, adorable girl. I'm utterly blessed to have her.

At the six-week check after Brianna's arrival a routine pap smear showed abnormal cells. This required an immediate procedure to minimise the cervical cancer risk – the first of many treatments that made it extremely unlikely I could ever have another child.

My marriage broke down after ten years, when Brianna was two and Cameron was five.

When I married Marcus in 2000, we were both aware and accepted that following treatment for cervical cancer and a recent cone biopsy, Cameron and Brianna wouldn't be joined by another sibling.

When I lost my seat in Parliament two years later, I started investigating my chances of conceiving with IVF. In my case, of course, it wasn't just the possibility of conceiving that was a challenge – it was my chances of carrying a baby. I was told in the unlikely event my eggs were okay, I would need what was left of my cervix stitched. This procedure carried with it a high risk of miscarriage.

I was very conscious of infertility treatment figures, I know how many people try and fail. The emotional rollercoaster most women and men go through while they're undergoing IVF, and the men too, because if the men are infertile and that's the reason they're doing IVF, is intense compared to a normal pregnancy.

While in Parliament I was involved in the subsequent framing of legislation around access to the fertility services. All those ethical issues I'd dealt with and policy making came to the fore as we considered our options. I was determined to try and felt strongly that Marcus deserved to have his own child.

So we started IVF and doing the hormone treatment, knowing the risks and the low potential for success. I became extremely ill from the injected hormones – they call it hyperstimulation, which puts you at risk of a stroke. The day before we were to have the eggs harvested, the clinic said the risk was too high and advised against proceeding.

I thought, I've come this far, I've tried this hard and this man deserves a child and so do I. I was absolutely adamant that I wanted to proceed and in the end the IVF specialists gave the go-ahead.

We had one implantation and Tess was conceived. Talk about a miracle. I was typically unwell through the early pregnancy – validation that the baby was well – and was really nervous about having the cervical suture at 12 weeks gestation. We were incredibly relieved that the baby was safe after the operation. I needed to stay in bed in hospital for a week then keep off my feet as much as possible to relieve pressure on what was left of my cervix — easier said than done with two young children.

Shortly after, I was feeling so unwell that I couldn't sleep at night, couldn't lie down, couldn't keep food down and felt stabbing pains. After a trip to Emergency and an ultrasound in hospital I was diagnosed with gall bladder disease, which could not be treated while I was pregnant. For an otherwise fit and healthy person, I couldn't believe how fragile I was whenever pregnant!

I went through the rest of the pregnancy so ill I thought neither of us would survive it. Throwing up was taking its toll on the cervical stitch and I prayed I could hold on long enough to deliver after 28 weeks — my minimum goal. With the help of friends and family I was able to keep off my feet and rest, which isn't something I do well.

So Tess Claire Davenport arrived on April Fool's Day 2004. Despite her prematurity she was healthy and breathing unassisted. She had difficulty feeding and we succeeded in avoiding her being intubated as the NICU and special care units of the hospital had an outbreak of Serratia bacteria, which resulted in some babies dying.

Luckily Tess grew in strength and is now . . . the most vivacious, happy, confident, beautiful girl. I had my gall bladder removed soon after she arrived. All's well that ends well.

There are many men and women facing similar issues and Bonnie Babes provides counselling which can really assist in the decision-making process.

So that's my story. That's why I'm helping Bonnie Babes and that's why I'm utterly committed, not just because of my own experience, but because so many people benefit from the Foundation's *work. There's nothing else comparable to support people suffering a loss, facing fertility issues, coping with premmies, living with a child with abnormalities.*

Also, Bonnie Babes provides support for people from generations past to accept that it's okay to grieve for their lost child.

It might have only been a fetus medically, but to a parent it's not, it's part of you, it's part of your life.

It is a national tragedy if a lack of funding continues to deny people the opportunity to have the best chance of having a family.

Research into the causes of loss, support for those who have tragically experienced loss and even acknowledgement of their loss needs to be supported by government, not just the community. After all, we all benefit from growing the population — babies we can save have the opportunity to contribute to our future.

Terri's story

Terri is Maree's mother and her story gives a look at the similarities between women the world and generations over who experience complications during their pregnancy and labour. Terri is a mother of six and grandmother of 19.

I was born in 1944 and I was just a little over 2 pounds [0.9 kilograms], so I wasn't dramatically small but, of course, there were no humidicribs or anything like that back then. Mum and Dad had a friend who was a local GP, they made up a little shoebox with cotton wool. Relatives, including two uncles who were doctors, who came to visit couldn't believe this.

In those days, people were a lot more inclined to actually get up and leave home and go and stay for a while if someone was sick, as my uncles did to nurse me. Pretty marvellous to think back over those times, and fortunately my family did help each other.

Mum had such a struggle to have had me. Dad was 44 and Mum was 38 and that was fairly late in those days. Dad was a farmer and life was tough.

I married Patrick Marley in 1966 and Maree was born in March 1968. Soon after I was pregnant again and it was a terrible shock to find I was carrying twins while [I was] in premature labour and Paul and John were born on 1 February 1969.

There were two dedicated nurses, one who was in charge of the nursery and another one who would stay longer than their shifts. When things were at their worst, and when the twins would stop breathing, they would sit there and gently rub them and get them going again.When you look at the monitors and things they have now, there was nothing like that then.

I used to dread the mornings because I knew one of us had to get out of bed and ring the hospital and find out if the twins were still alive, it was really stressful. But we were terribly lucky, because we had families around us and we had both sets of grandparents nearby.

The twins were in hospital until they were almost one, by this time I was heavily pregnant with Andrew, who was born in May 1970. I went on to have Damian in January 1972 and Helen in July 1974. Family has always been the centre of our lives and we're so proud to see the great parents our children have become and enjoy our grandchildren immensely.

Learning to cope with pregnancy complications

Complications during pregnancy can be frightening and confusing. Routine check-ups and scans will help to alert your healthcare provider to anything that might not seem right with the pregnancy. If you have been diagnosed with any of the aforementioned complications it is important to:

Stay informed and tell your doctor if anything is troubling you
- Many women have a feeling that something is not right. Always act on this instinct if you are worried about any change in your pregnancy or your baby's development. It is important, if you are diagnosed with a specific complication, to learn as much as you can to help understand the condition and learn about what you can do to alleviate symptoms or risks. Being well-informed will also help you make any decisions that may affect the health of yourself or your baby.

Keep well, stay well
- Pregnancy complications are the major cause of preventable newborn deaths in Australia. Healthy diet, regular exercise and knowing some of the risk factors that can be avoided are essential for a healthy and developing pregnancy.

Support groups, counselling and support networks
- If you have been diagnosed with a particular complication it can sometimes help to be in contact with mothers or parents with a similar complication. Knowing what to expect and being aware that other parents might be experiencing the same thing can help alleviate some of the stress caused by uncertainties or worries about the pregnancy or birth complications.

Common Questions

How can I prevent pregnancy complications?

Keeping healthy by eating a wide range of fresh food and maintaining a regular exercise program that is suitable to your level of fitness and the stage of your pregnancy is essential for the wellbeing of yourself and your baby. It has also been proven that an adequate intake of folic acid (part of the B group vitamins) should be taken by all women of childbearing age who are thinking of having children. Studies have shown that an adequate amount of maternal intake of folic acid can reduce the rate of fetal neural tube defects, such as spina bifida and anencephaly, and other congenital malformations by as much as 70 per cent. Stopping smoking is one of the best things you can do. Consult with your doctor or healthcare provider about maintaining and improving the health of yourself and your baby. Women who have suffered from severe early onset pre-eclampsia may benefit from taking a low-dose aspirin in their next pregnancy to prevent a recurrence of the disorder. If you are not yet pregnant, check your immunity to rubella and get vaccinated if necessary. In autumn, get a flu shot, which is safe in pregnancy.

Can some pregnancy complications be treated or cured?

This depends on the type of condition that might come up in the various antenatal checks and scans. For example, the diagnosis of pre-eclampsia can minimise any further pregnancy complications relating to this condition. If the placenta appears to be lying low at the 20-week ultrasound, the doctor will book another ultrasound at around 32 weeks gestation. Reassuringly, 80 per cent of placentas that were low at 20 weeks are no longer low-lying by 32 weeks gestation, in which case there is no further risk of placenta praevia. If the placenta remains low at 32 weeks, then the diagnosis of placenta praevia is made. The doctor will need to plan how the baby is birthed (which is likely to be a caesarian section), and may admit you for the last few weeks of pregnancy since the risk of a bleed may be high.

Should I be worried about bleeding or spotting during my pregnancy?

Call your doctor or healthcare provider straightaway, even if the bleeding seems to have stopped. While it may turn out to be something minor, it could be a sign of a serious problem. Your doctor will give you an examination to make sure you and your baby are fine and to rule out any complications.

I feel like I'm having contractions but my baby is not yet full-term. What should I do?

If you feel contractions and you still have a way to go with your pregnancy, contact your doctor and healthcare provider immediately. It is quite common to feel contractions towards the end of a pregnancy. If they are weak and irregular, and if they go away after a short period of time, they are unlikely to indicate preterm labour. However, if you do have any concerns, always contact your doctor or healthcare provider.

Will pregnancy complications in one pregnancy happen in following pregnancies?

If you are at high-risk for particular health conditions or there are genetic disorders that need to be considered in any future pregnancies, it is important to consult your doctor before making the decision to follow through with another pregnancy. Depending on the condition, the monitoring and treatment of subsequent pregnancies might involve extra scans and blood tests to reassure you throughout the pregnancy that all is progressing well. A condition such as pre-eclampsia in one pregnancy will not necessarily affect subsequent pregnancies or if it does, it generally occurs in a milder form.

If my health is severely affected by a pregnancy complication, will I have to choose between my baby's health or my health?

If a complication develops during your pregnancy your doctor or healthcare provider will advise you of what needs to be done to either limit the effects of the complication or eliminate any further risk to either you or your baby.

Resources

Australian Action on Pre-eclampsia Inc. (AAPEC)

Australian Action on Pre-eclampsia Inc. is an association incorporated in Victoria. It is a voluntary organisation set up to provide support and information to families who suffer from pre-eclampsia.

PO Box 29, Carlton South, VIC 3053

Phone: (03) 9330 0441

To Our Little Champions

TAMMY AND DANIEL

Take care of each other in all of your travels and remember wherever you go, we're both with you.

In our hearts you shall always remain; every day that passes will be one day closer to seeing you both again.

Until that time our memories of you both shall always be treasured deep in our hearts.

With our eternal love forever,

Mummy and Daddy.

Chapter 8

Something's come up on the ultrasound

Antenatal testing is a routine part of pregnancy, providing parents with information about how their baby is progressing, reassuring the healthcare provider that the pregnancy is low or minimal risk and removing the anxiety that some parents, particularly older or at-risk mothers, may feel during their pregnancy. Parents hope for confirmation that their baby is healthy.

Although most babies are healthy, for some parents the result of an antenatal test will bring the news that their baby may have a serious problem. Despite the advances in medical science, with the diagnosis of a fetal abnormality, often little can be done to cure the baby or correct the problem that might be developing.

Shock, numbness, confusion and fear are all common responses to this overwhelming news. Guilt is another feeling that can surface in that the parents will try to pinpoint an event or incident that might have contributed to the development of the abnormality. In most cases, there is nothing the parents have done to cause the condition, or could have done to prevent it.

If you have been told that there is something wrong with your baby, take the time to consider all aspects of the diagnosis and your options in what this will mean for you, your family and the potential child. Ask your doctor or genetic counsellor what the effects and consequences of the abnormality are, what quality of life your child would expect, and what other families' experiences are in caring for their children with similar problems.

Becoming informed about your baby's condition is critical in the early stages of the diagnosis. It will also be important to examine your beliefs and how you will continue with the pregnancy, if you decide to do so. To help make these decisions, be as certain as you can about the diagnosis and seek expert opinion and further tests if necessary. Learn all you can about the symptoms of the conditions and the long-term effects.

It also helps to talk to other parents who have faced a similar situation. This way you can get information from people who really understand and can explain how they deal with their day-to-day life, medical costs and any other practical considerations that might need to be taken into account.

Start building a support network among your close friends and family. Talking to someone else you can trust, other than your partner, can often open up new possibilities in tackling your dilemma and also provide a different subjective point of view on how to approach your decisions.

Carefully consider the impact on your family and the baby. You may want to consider your family's needs and the needs of your baby. Think about the possible risks and benefits with each choice you face. There is the consideration of the suffering or level of pain or discomfort that your baby will experience as they get older. Always consider the impact a baby with a severe medical condition will have on the relationship with your partner.

Also look within yourself to get an instinctual feel as to what decision or choice you want to make. There is always the emotional part of the decision to be considered. Don't forget to consider how this will affect your personal plans and dreams for the future.

Because of the shock of receiving bad news, it may be difficult to remember what is said when you hear the news. Writing down information to look at in your own time can be helpful. Depending on the condition that your baby has there might be a lot of information available or if the condition is rare there might be limited information. Again your doctor will provide you with more detailed information and contacts.

Deciding to continue with a pregnancy when an abnormality is detected

You may have been told that your baby's chances of survival are poor, or that your baby will die. There may be uncertainty about what will happen at or after their birth. Because of this uncertainty the pregnancy can become a very precious time for you and your partner.

If this is your situation, you might want to make certain preparations. It may be upsetting imagining the worst, but some parents say that preparing for their baby's death gave them something to focus on. It allowed them some control over what was going to happen.

If you know your baby is certain to die after birth, you may not want a medical team to keep them alive for too long or intervene unnecessarily. You might prefer to care for your baby yourself with the support of your medical team. You should be allowed all the time that you want to spend with your baby. You can ask family and friends to visit you after the birth or you might want to take your baby home (if the baby's health can withstand this).

You may also wish to consider funeral/memorial arrangements if there is a possibility that your baby will not survive being born. Although this will be difficult, making arrangements and plans means that you are involved in making decisions about your baby – this is your right as a parent. It might also be important to you to think about mementoes and keepsakes to remind you of your pregnancy and your baby.

If you wish to continue the pregnancy but are unsure you want to care for a very ill or dying baby, options include relinquishing the baby for adoption or arranging a planned period of foster care.

There is no way to tell how long your pregnancy and birth will last. It can depend on what is wrong with the baby, the number of babies and your health. There are no time guarantees. Your medical support team will want to monitor your pregnancy closely as it nears term, making sure that complications do not develop. Always make sure that you understand all the information relayed to you by the medical staff to help you with any decisions that need to be made.

It can sometimes be difficult letting others know about your decision to continue on with the pregnancy, because some people may wish to influence your decision as they try to minimise your heartache and pain or because of their personal beliefs or experiences. People will also question your ability to cope with a challenged child once it is born. Stay firm with your decision and don't feel that family and friends can force or sway your final decision to go through with the pregnancy. This is your and your partner's decision based on all the information you have gathered from your doctor and medical team. Make sure you are surrounded by people who support your decision so that you can continue and focus on the path that you have chosen.

Waiting for the birth of your baby will involve a complex range of emotions and feelings. During the pregnancy your baby may still be alive. Some people have said that this time spent with their baby before birth has been valuable and precious as the baby is still being cared for and is safe. Sometimes this period of waiting helps people work through some of their grief and shock at the news of the condition of their baby.

This time can also be emotionally difficult to deal with. Everyday tasks might seem difficult to get through or you may want to limit social contact with others, keeping only a close circle of friends and family around you. Finding strong support is the key to coping with fluctuating emotions and moods. If at any time there is a feeling of overwhelming, disabling grief or despair, seeking professional help or counselling can be invaluable to help you continue through the term of your pregnancy.

Deciding to end a pregnancy when an abnormality is detected

If you have made the decision to end a wanted pregnancy because of problems detected in your baby, it is normal to feel extreme and painful emotions. You may also be worried about what you are about to go through and the sense of 'what if', not knowing if your decision is the 'right' one. There is no right or wrong: be guided by the information you receive from your medical support team and the decisions you have made.

This experience won't be easy but knowing very clearly about all the options available is crucial to help cope with the decision made.

The idea of causing harm to your child may go against your sense of what is right or what you feel is natural. However, as you weigh your options and the possible pain and suffering that your baby might endure, it may seem like the lesser of two difficult choices.

There are a number of methods of pregnancy termination used when a baby has either died or is still alive. You will need to consult with your doctor or healthcare provider to find out what method is suitable for your case. One method is the induction of labour, where birth is induced. After the baby is born, make sure that time is spent with them to create a moment in time as a complete family. With the birth of the baby an autopsy and genetic studies can be done to determine the nature and full complications of the diagnosed abnormalities. The information gathered can also be used to let you know of any genetic or hereditary risks that may be carried over to future pregnancies. If the gestational age of your baby is under 15 weeks then a dilation and curettage (D&C) will be done. In this procedure a complete autopsy cannot be performed, however genetic studies can still be done to provide further information about your baby's condition.

If you have ended the pregnancy it may be difficult letting others know about your decision. Focus on your decision and the reasons why you have made it and try to protect yourself from any insensitive comments by surrounding yourself with close friends and family. You will feel a range of emotions associated with grief – anger, guilt and a sense of responsibility. Allow your feelings to surface, discuss them openly with your partner and make sure you grieve in a way that is right for you to help you recover from this experience.

Lucy's story

Lucy was born without one of her ears; there is no hole, there is nothing, just a bit of tissue; and she was born with a really severe club foot, so she was in plaster when she was 12 hours old, from her toes to her hip.

I think I went into shock. It was weeks later the Child and Maternal Health Nurse, she could see I was struggling, said to me that I had to grieve for the perfect baby – because I had produced a baby that wasn't perfect.

I know that's not a loss, and I would never compare it. But it just gave me an inkling of the feelings that you would go through if the pregnancy hadn't resulted in perfection, which we all expect our babies to be.

She [the midwife] couldn't find the right word to describe an imperfect baby. It was awful, it was like she had big boots on and I had to say, 'Don't talk about my little baby in this rough, offhand way.'

I just wanted to hide Lucy and I felt as though everyone was watching me, they probably weren't, but I felt like that. Here is me trying to hide and protect this baby who hasn't got all its bits . . .

When the nurse said to me, You must grieve, you must grieve for the perfect baby, and the feeling of failure and the blame . . . to this day I think back to the day I was scraping paint off the back of the door and I could remember it getting in my mouth and I think to myself, I wonder if it was that day that I ate some lead paint and that's what did it?

It's very hard if you have a child who is born, I hate to say 'not perfect', because she is perfect to me.

Robert and Danielle's story

Danielle and her husband, AFL star Robert Harvey
have always given their support to the Bonnie Babes
Foundation. They are the parents of three young children
but the road to parenthood, for them, has been hard and
not quite how they expected it to happen.

Their dream was to have four kids and when they were reasonably young they made the decision to have a family. Their first child, Connor, was conceived very quickly and the pregnancy and birth went well, apart from Danielle's extreme morning sickness. They assumed that any other pregnancies would be just as easy and straightforward.

I fell pregnant straightaway again [after Connor], had the morning sickness again and I was very excited, we were right on plan . . . we were going to have four children by the time I was 36. The pregnancy after Connor was an ectopic one [outside the womb]. Our second successful pregnancy was Remi.

We were telling everyone I was pregnant with our third child. We were on holidays; I was 14 weeks pregnant and started spotting, so we flew home. The baby had died the week before. I was devastated. Some people don't recognise a miscarriage at 14 weeks as being an actual child. But believe me, when you have felt the sickness, or the movement of that life inside of you, that's something between you and your husband, that is something you definitely have to deal with in order to move on and have another healthy pregnancy. This was our first miscarriage after two successful pregnancies.

Shortly afterwards I fell pregnant again, once again quite easily. We went and had the scans to make sure everything was fine. I had a lot of spotting and a lot of sickness. They thought I had a gallstone problem, so I had a scan for that.

After the scan, Danielle and Robert were told to contact their doctor urgently and have another scan. The second follow-up scan revealed something that shocked the young parents to the core.

I was told that the pregnancy, while proceeding and the baby was alive, had horrific genetic problems. This was our third miscarriage.

I remember Rob coming in from training and I had just been told that we had lost another baby [our fifth miscarriage]. The disappointment on Rob's face was horrific. That was just a little bit harder for us because we had to have a delivery. I'll never forget seeing this still baby on the monitor.

From Robert's point of view, it was the worst one because it was the one you saw, it was delivered, it was real. It was really hard to see Danielle go through that with a delivery and the pressure, and get no result at the end . . .

Suffering a sixth miscarriage was another blow for Danielle and Robert who were trying to fulfil their dream of a big family. Luckily they carried Alyssa full-term and she became their much-loved third child.

Again, a good support team was crucial for Danielle and Robert pulling through this tragedy. It also brought home to Danielle that many women do suffer in silence when faced with a devastating complication during pregnancy.

One of my greatest supports was my nanna, who had lost two children, at six and a half months pregnant. I really feel that it's something you can't understand until you've experienced it yourself to a degree.

I sort of got the impression, which I think a lot of women get, that people just thought I should just get over it . . . but I truly felt in every ounce of my body that there was someone missing and that this [having more children] was something I had to do.

I don't believe that you can go through that sort of loss or that sort of grief without some sort of help, to have someone who's not family talk to you.

Learning to cope with congenital malformations

Find good support networks
Gather good friends and close family around you at this time. You need to feel that you can be open about what is going on for you, your partner and your baby and to grieve as you feel you need to. Support is crucial to help validate whatever decision you make regarding the outcome of your pregnancy. Ask your doctor or healthcare provider to give

you some contacts for support groups that are relevant to your situation. It often helps to hear other people's stories as to how they have coped.

Information is the key
Once you have received the diagnosis and confirmation of the condition, find out as much as you can to help assist you with any decisions you will have to make over the remainder of your pregnancy. If something is not completely clear, ask your doctor or healthcare provider to explain.

Understand how to make decisions calmly
In a crisis, the skills of clear decision-making can be difficult to implement. When faced with stressful decisions where the outcome is uncertain, it is natural to attempt to avoid making a decision, hoping the problem will go away. You need to have confidence in yourself to go forward, and believe that you can make the best decision possible for the time. Acknowledge that the choice is yours and your partner's and write down the options that you feel are available to you. For each choice, list the positives and the negatives. If there are a number of options on your list, eliminate the ones that you are not able to consider or don't want to follow through on. Always listen to your heart and gut instinct when settling on the final choice and decision.

Common Questions

I am in my forties. What is the risk and the statistics of Down syndrome babies?

At age 35, the risk of Down syndrome is one in 350. Every year of additional age increases the risk. By age 45 the risk is one in 20.

Is folic acid helpful for pregnancy to decrease abnormalities in babies?

Taking 500 micrograms a day of folic acid for at least three months prior to pregnancy decreases the risk of spina bifida by 70 per cent. In absolute terms, however, the overall risk drops from 0.3 per cent to 0.1 per cent, so those who do not take folic acid are still unlikely to have a baby with spina bifida. There are lots of other things doctors can recommend to improve your chance of a healthy pregnancy. This is called 'preconception care'.

Can the doctors be wrong? Is it possible that the baby will survive and live a normal life?

In a very low percentage of cases, the diagnosis can turn out to be wrong. Sometimes the condition that was diagnosed was actually less severe than previously thought. If you are concerned about the initial diagnosis it is an option to get a second opinion.

What do I say to people when they ask how the baby is?

Depending on how you have adjusted to the news and also who you are with and how your mood is, your response may vary. Some days you might not want to answer the question, other days you might feel more confident. Don't feel that you have to tell people everything if you don't want to. Everyone handles traumatic news differently. You can ask a close friend to let people know what is happening with the pregnancy.

What are my rights and options if my baby lives and needs medical care?

This is an important consideration if your baby is born and requires medical intervention. There are many questions that you can ask your doctor and medical staff looking after your baby. You will need to be clear about how far you will pursue medical intervention, the support the medical team can provide, what the financial costs are for continued management and the long-term effects of any medical treatment that is used on your baby.

How will I look after a child with special needs?

Depending on the baby's problems, parenting a child with specific difficulties will be challenging and stressful. Make sure your support networks are strong and that you are able to have some support from family and friends. Support groups for specific conditions can be helpful to put you in contact with organisations, counselling and respite care to assist at the times when you feel you might not be coping. Always ask for help if you need it.

Resources

Suggested reading:

Ilse, S., *Precious Lives, Painful Choices: a prenatal decision-making guide,*
Wintergreen Press, 1993

Brock and Dejay
OUR PRECIOUS LITTLE BOYS

Together we will always be – for all of eternity
Until our family once again
In our hearts you shall both remain.
Our cute little boys, you fought so long
We're proud of you both for being so strong.
We can't explain the pain inside
though it's something we cannot hide.
When we held you close to our hearts
We didn't feel so many miles apart.
Our twin little boys that could never be
You're the cutest boys we will ever see.
Until we meet in the stars one night
Forever hold each other tight.

Chapter 9

What can we do, how can we help?

Losing a baby is an experience no parent wants to go through, yet many have to face. A neonatal loss, miscarriage or stillbirth often leaves friends and family not knowing what to say or how to react, and this can make a very difficult time even harder to cope with. Sometimes people say nothing for fear of upsetting the grieving parents, sometimes people can say something that is unintentionally insensitive or hurtful because they are trying to lessen the pain and suffering that someone is going through.

Advice for family and friends

At this painful time in the parents' lives, they want to talk about their baby's death and they need to feel that they are able to openly talk about how they are feeling and their concerns regarding what the immediate future holds for them.

Family and friends can help and support the parents by encouraging them to talk and by being a sympathetic and mindful listener. The parents also need to feel that others are remembering and honouring the baby they have lost. Ignoring the death and the grief does not make the pain go away or assist with healing. The approach of 'look on the bright side, things will get better' is not helpful when people are gripped by the depths of despair. Some people try to ignore the subject in order to minimise the amount of pain by not mentioning what has happened. Don't protect grieving parents from their pain; find ways to help them face their grief. In most cases, it hurts the parents if people ignore what has happened to them and this type of reaction can be interpreted as others being insensitive or uncaring. It can also feel, to the parents, that someone is trying to lessen the importance of the loss of a child. The parents are parents who have lost a child and will forever see themselves as parents without a child – and that child is a very real part of their lives. Get involved, be willing and interested in hearing about their experiences and also respect the parents' wishes in however they choose to remember their baby.

Creating trust and support

The most important help you can offer is compassion and good listening skills. Allow the grieving parents to talk and express their grief in whichever way they need. This may include crying, fits of anger, screaming, laughing and expressions of guilt or regret.

People are very vulnerable to the criticism and judgment of others. People who are grieving need to know that they can be themselves and relax with their feelings. They need to feel that they can openly cry. Everyone's experience of grief is different so judging or expressing that they need to behave a certain way in order to heal will make them less likely to share their feelings with you. Don't push people to talk. If sitting in silence is what is needed then follow the parents' cues as to where they are up to in dealing with their grief. Don't forget the power of human touch. Holding a person's hand or giving them a hug, if they want one, is a way of offering emotional support.

Providing support for the parents

The support that you give the parents doesn't have to be a big gesture; it just needs to show the parents that they, and their baby, are in your thoughts. In the first few days make contact with a call, a sympathy card, flowers or a visit, offer support if you are able to.

Some suggestions to help you comfort and care include:

Listen, listen, listen

You can talk about the death and about their baby. Be brave and ask questions if the parents want to talk. Most parents need and want to talk about their baby, their hopes and dreams and their child who has died, even if it was a miscarriage. Always ask if people feel like talking and take your lead from what the parents seem to need.

Empathy

Realise that the parents are sad because they miss the baby who can never be replaced by anyone else. The baby is a glimpse into a particular future and now this expectation of what was meant to happen no longer exists.

Acknowledge the baby

Say the baby's name out loud and if they have been named or ask about the baby's name. This can be really valuable to the parents that someone is acknowledging the baby as a little person and confirms the baby's existence, cementing the reality that they are parents.

Accept there is nothing you can say that will make people feel better

Don't jump in to fill the sadness with topics that will take the parents away from their grief. Try not to tell them about your grief experience, just listen to theirs, and don't compare their grief with yours or anyone else's as this can come across as suggesting that their grief is not an individual one. Some well-meaning friends and family may try to structure the grief process by suggesting that there is a right and wrong way to grieve. Rather than being constructive, this approach will make the parents feel inadequate and that their grief is not completely valid.

Practical help

Offer to do things like clean the house, do some grocery shopping, cook some meals, weed the garden, babysit children. Think of chores that will allow the grieving parents to focus on coping with their grief rather than feeling overwhelmed by things they need to get done.

Remember the parents' loss and keep in contact with them around anniversaries

Once the initial shock lessens and people go back to their normal lives, parents included, it is very easy to forget anniversaries of passing. There is nothing more heartwarming than to receive a card or call on these particular days. The parents will feel that they are not alone in their time of sorrow.

Dee Dee's story

Diane Dunleavy is a loving wife and caring mother to her two children, Bonnie and Bailey. Many know her as Dee Dee, the Gold 104.3 radio personality. She has been a Patron of the Bonnie Babes Foundation for a number of years.

Bonnie was born in 1995, which is around the time of my association with Bonnie Babes and it was just a coincidence with the name — it just fell into place, like it was meant to be.

I had only just returned to work from maternity leave, Bonnie was seven months old and a friend at another radio station, her baby was stillborn. A lot of colleagues at work went to the funeral and to see grown men who were all radio announcers, guys who always have a line for this and a line for that and everything is all waffle or laughed off, to see them coming back into work absolutely shattered and describing the size of the coffin.

It was heartbreaking and you don't want anyone to go through that.

I have girlfriends who have had miscarriages. My best friend was 46 and wanted to have another baby. She has a 13-year-old and a three-year-old, but miscarried her third child.

People said to her, 'Well, that's for the best', 'That's God's message', 'You shouldn't be having one at your age!'

I rang her while she was still in the hospital and I asked, 'Was it a boy or a girl?'

'It was a little girl' she said. 'You know you are the first person that has asked me that?'

I said, 'What was her name?'

Again she said no one had even asked. No one had talked about the baby as though she was a person, and I find this really the saddest thing.

Only through knowing that it is not something you can't talk about . . . you have got to be gentle and you have to be sympathetic and understanding, but don't not talk about it.

It's amazing how many times you're touched by it. I have another girlfriend, and I mentioned Bonnie Babes to her and she said, 'I lost two babies, I lost twins.'

She said that she'd never talked about it before. She got to 24 weeks and had gone for one of her scans. The doctor just said to her, 'When did you know they were dead? Didn't you feel they were dead?'

She was so shocked; she hadn't realised at that point that they were gone. It was as though they were almost accusing her that somehow she should have realised and raised an alarm. She didn't know, she was a young girl, she didn't realise they were dead. She has never talked about it.

My mum has a friend who, in the early 1960s, got to full-term and gave birth, but the baby was dead and they took it away. She never saw it; they just took it.

Chapter 10

What do you tell the children?

One of the most difficult tasks that parents can face in life is explaining to their children why the baby they were expecting to be joining their family has died. Often parents are faced with difficult questions like – 'But how did our baby die?' 'Where is it now?' 'Will I die too?' In many cases we may not have answers to these questions. Where medical explanations are available they may be far too complicated for a child to comprehend. At such a stressful time for the parents, it is important to distinguish between unburdening your grief onto the children versus sharing what happened. One way to help is to make yourself feel more calm when you are about to tell your child. If you find yourself getting upset, slow down your words, take a deep breath, focus on an object to regain your sense of focus, and start again. Being able to trust an adult is a vital factor in how well children deal with trauma and that trust is based on honest and open communication. It is very important that children believe they have permission to ask questions that will be answered honestly and in a way that makes sense.

It is important to include children in all aspects of life and death in a way that is developmentally appropriate. In the past it was assumed children did not understand grief and death so it was best to exclude them to 'spare them' unnecessary emotional distress. However, recent literature points out that by such exclusion we run the risk of children suffering emotional trauma. This occurs where incorrect assumptions are made by the child in an effort to make sense of what has happened when factual information is not available. For example, if in the case of threatened miscarriage, when children have been told they must be 'good' while Mum is not well: if the baby subsequently dies, the child may believe they are responsible for this event because they are not 'good' all the time.

Telling your children

Parents often express frustration and reluctance when faced with explaining the death of a baby to surviving children. Most parents are concerned with protecting their children and with this aim, may, in fact, offer no explanation. This is sometimes an attractive option for parents as it saves them having to relive the experience when retelling the story.

When a baby dies, or indeed when any family member dies, it is important to check with children regarding what they understand has happened. Once you have established their level of knowledge, you may wish to ask them if they have any questions about the situation. When these questions have been answered, to ensure the information you have provided has been heard correctly, ask the child again what they now understand. Depending on the issue you have addressed you may want to ask – 'Can you tell me what

I said?' or 'Now you tell me how the baby died.' Talking about the death of a baby whilst you and your child are in a play situation (with building blocks, drawing materials, playdough etc) also helps the child to listen better and ask questions. The intensity of a face-to-face talk may at times prevent effective communication and lead to more upset over such a sensitive and sad subject.

When answering a child's questions regarding the death of a baby or the death of any loved person it is important the child has heard the adults imparting this information correctly. Too often, both children and adults will misunderstand or process only some of the information provided. This can leave them more confused and perhaps even fearful. Uncertainty is often the cause of emotional distress. It is well documented that whenever information is presented following a traumatic event, difficulty in processing and retaining this information occurs. It is of vital importance to ask a child to repeat what has been said to check that there is no harmful misinterpretation.

A child's view of grief

The grief process for adults *and* children is one that unfolds over time. Children who may at first seem unmoved by a death may then evolve into anger, sadness and resentment. Adults need to be aware of the way children are processing their grief and be ready to act on their needs at this tragic time. Many parents may require validation that the choices they are making in including their children are appropriate. Parents are encouraged to let children take part in the grieving process and, in particular, express their fear and anger. It is useful to be aware of the differing ways we handle grief, and that as adults we may not be ready for the grief of others when ours is so consuming. It can help to 'stop, slow down, and connect with others (even in their grief)', to help manage your own. In the face of such adversity, ensure it does not consume you; it can even help you to connect with others and to the baby who has died. You may at times need to be alone in your grief, whilst at other times be willing to share your grief with trusted others.

Children understand death in different ways depending on their age and developmental level. Pre-school children view death as reversible – a temporary state. School-age children are more concrete in their cognitive abilities to conceptualise death. However, there is still an ego protective function operating where they believe that if they are clever enough they will avoid death. Adolescents are capable of abstract reasoning and understand the finality of death, although they may be reluctant to share their thoughts about death with their parents or other adults. Access to a counsellor may be helpful here.

Saying goodbye to a brother or sister

There are some ways to help your child say goodbye to their little brother or sister. If the child feels involved in an activity such as creating something of their own to give to the baby, this may help to validate the baby's existence in their mind.

Mourning rituals can be extremely powerful in providing an opportunity to outwardly express sorrow. They can also give meaning and structure to feelings. In addition they provide the opportunity to 'do' something when we feel powerless and vulnerable. The same applies to children and the following activities can assist you with setting up some rituals with your children. Some examples include drawing a picture for the baby, writing a special story or prayer, planting something in the garden. Ask your child for their own ideas.

The service

Offer the children an opportunity to be involved in any service for the baby. Some children will choose to write the baby a letter, draw a picture, read a poem or let go of some balloons at an appropriate time in the service. Such items can be placed in the baby's coffin or alternatively kept in a memory box.

Special garden

Identify a section of your garden as a place to design a special memory garden where a tree or rose can be planted, statue or water feature erected or annuals planted for ongoing work in memory of your child's brother or sister. You can be as creative as you wish in designing this special place where quiet time can also be spent. If you plan to move to another home consider buying a plant that you can take cuttings from to recreate the garden at another location. These cuttings can also be offered as gifts to grandparents and close friends in memory of the baby.

Memory box

Go shopping as a family for a special memory box where copies of letters or drawings for the baby can be kept. On the anniversary of your baby's birth (even if it is also the day your baby died) you may wish to buy a small gift and place it in the memory box.

Write a letter

You can write a letter to your child that they can put into their memory box and keep returning to at a later stage in their grieving process to reassure themselves. This letter can include things about your child being brave and letting them know that they are a strong support in this difficult time.

Gifts to share

At Christmas children can buy a present for their little brother or sister and donate it to a charity or a 'wishing tree' set up in some department stores. Or Easter eggs can be bought and donated to other children in need. These gifts are bought with siblings in mind, although it can be applied to any loved family member who has died.

Star babies

Several years ago the Bonnie Babes Foundation was offered a star in recognition of the work carried out by the Foundation. Parents have found it useful in the past to use this star as a focus for children when there is a need to think of the baby having a place to 'be' — a star where lots of babies live. This is very useful for families with spiritual foundations where the parent and child may want to say a prayer together outside, looking to the heavens and focusing on their special star.

Helping your children after a loss

Parents often seek and welcome consultation and advice about how to deal with talking to surviving children. Trained counsellors can be invaluable at this time, offering reassurance to parents and guidance regarding the need to be honest with children, to answer their questions and to include them in the grief process. If you would like to talk to a trained counsellor regarding your grief and be offered options for referral to assist your children, contact the Bonnie Babes Foundation.

Following are some activities that you can do with your child to help them deal with their loss and to also create a positive memory of their brother or sister.

- Prepare pens, paper, glue, textured materials, paint, etc, and invite your child to create something for the baby. This could be a picture, mobile, a painting or a window decoration.
- Invite your child to write a letter or poem, or compose his or her very own song.
- Write a story for the baby.
- Write the baby's life story, telling how the family felt about this baby.
- Design the baby's special garden and write a list of the plants needed to create the garden.
- Design a special Christmas ornament to be placed on the Christmas tree each year. Mark the year on the ornament and watch as they make your tree more special as years go by. Adding this ornament each year also includes your special baby in the joy of every Christmas morning as children open their presents.

Other ways of helping your child cope with the loss is by creating an environment where they will feel comfortable asking or talking about their brother or sister. Creating a scrapbook, celebrating a birthday or observing the anniversary of their sibling's death can also help them hold on to some memories of their own.

Resources

McKay, P. *How Do We Tell the Kids?*
Bonnie Babes Foundation, *Talking to Children about Grief and Loss*

Chapter 11

A medical perspective

Doctors, nurses and allied health staff are on the other side of the events that come up for parents and their babies. Medical staff usually work tirelessly to give the best possible care in a wide and varied range of situations. They are not only 'medicos' but are people who are at the coalface when dealing with the pain and suffering that the parents can go through. The following stories give an insight into how health care professionals deal with the rawness of emotion that they are confronted with and also feel themselves when faced with the heartache parents experience when they lose their baby.

Dr Cindy Pan

Dr Cindy Pan is an author and was a long-time panellist on Beauty and the Beast *as well as appearing on* The Panel *and* The Glasshouse. *She now writes several columns, including a weekly health column in* Body and Soul *for Sunday papers all over Australia and a regular column on relationships in the* Women's Weekly *in Singapore and Malaysia. Cindy has been a Patron of the Bonnie Babes Foundation for a number of years. Cindy is the mother of two young boys, Anton and Jeremy.*

Cindy explains that being a GP and seeing a range of women either earnestly trying to prevent (or end) a pregnancy or desperately trying to have a baby always amazed her. On becoming pregnant herself, she became ever more aware of just how precious and unexpected life is and how falling pregnant and carrying a pregnancy to full-term is not something that should be taken for granted.

'In general practice I often found that I'd have one woman coming in wanting a termination and the very next woman would be coming in with fertility problems, desperate to have a baby . . . I'd be filling out forms to recommend someone regarding adoption and I would think . . . *Oh gosh, I wish I could swap these two people around: one desperately wants a baby and can't have one and the other is pregnant and really doesn't want to be . . .*'

Again in her practice, Cindy was able to calmly see women who had miscarriages but it wasn't until she had one herself that things became personal.

'I saw quite a lot of women who had miscarriages. I suppose I thought of miscarriage as being obviously very distressing but not necessarily so very tragic, except in certain cases, for example where the woman was older and didn't have any children and had had serious difficulties falling pregnant in the first place.

'I had a miscarriage in between [my sons] Anton and Jeremy. I think if it had been my first pregnancy . . . I'm not saying it didn't upset me, of course it did . . . but I think if it had been my very first pregnancy it would have been a lot more alarming and distressing. I suppose because I'd already had one perfectly successful pregnancy and I knew that according to the statistics miscarriage is so common, I was upset but perhaps not so devastated as I might otherwise have been.

'Fertility is one of those things where until you've been pregnant you've got no idea how fertile you might be. Having had a career and having had so many patients – even some very young women – who had had difficulty falling pregnant, I thought, *Oh, you know, that'll have to be me for sure.*

'But as it turned out, I fell pregnant straightaway and the pregnancy went really well; I didn't really have any serious problems at all.

'To my mind, a successful pregnancy and delivery is when you get a healthy baby, however that might occur.

'But I truly believe that even if you're only a parent for a brief moment it has meaning, doesn't it? I do feel so fortunate to have been given the opportunity to be a mother that I think, that just to have lived what you've lived is a real gift, isn't it?'

Dr Bennett Sheridan

At 19 years of age, Dr Bennett Sheridan completed a Bonnie Babes grief counsellor's training course. He completed it the second time when he became the Medical Secretary of the Bonnie Babes Foundation's medical board, which was over 10 year ago.

Bennett was working with grief and loss in palliative care and became interested in the aspect of grief and loss in perinatal care – the other end of the spectrum. He chose to do his undergraduate research in perinatal medicine in neonatal intensive care units. It was here that his interest in working with families and premature babies came to the fore. He was lucky to be able to spend his time working with families and seeing how they coped and dealt with looking after their premature babies in intensive care.

'It gave me the practical and emotional insight into what was required having a baby in an intensive care unit. [I also saw] the utter and thorough disturbance of somebody's life having a baby in intensive care. I remember the lives of siblings being thrown into turmoil, fathers taking extended leave from jobs, losing jobs in one example from rather an uncaring employer. That impact on life outside the nursery, how some families can spend so much time sitting with their baby in the nursery that their life outside the nursery falls apart.

'Interestingly, on the other side of that, you can see babies in the nursery where you don't see the family much, and medical staff would ask, "Where is this family, their baby's ventilated in intensive care, why aren't they seeing the baby more often, why aren't they sitting here with the baby?"

'The reality is they have probably got three other kids at home who they are looking after plus whatever makes up the rest of their lives . . .'

Bennett succinctly explains that medical practitioners do need to look beyond the things that they might see and judge in these stressful situations, with parents dealing with the life or death of their baby.

'It is too easy for health practitioners to judge the actions of the parent, particularly how involved or otherwise they may seem with their baby. You form an opinion of what is average by seeing hundreds of parents and then suddenly someone's outside that average and you may think they're behaving incorrectly. However, this behaviour might be normal for them.'

Bennett is also able to look at both sides of how parents and doctors react in such highly emotional and tense situations that can arise in the neonatal intensive care unit. Some health professionals are able to deal with things comfortably because of their personality, experience, their background.

'I know some professionals are uncomfortable dealing with difficult and highly emotive circumstances themselves; they try to avoid it, but sometimes you can't.

'From the other side of the ward, it is extremely hard to walk into a room of two parents, usually two grandparents, aunty, uncle, upwards of ten people at times, and take the floor and break bad news, sometimes terrible news. That's an extremely difficult thing, an extremely stressful thing and some people don't cope [with giving this bad news], and their own anxiety comes across as something unfavourable and they can seem abrupt or arrogant.'

There is some training in place to deal with these difficult situations, such as role-playing, but as Bennett says, it is not the same as dealing with the real event and dealing with how grieving people react to the doctors and the hospital environment.

Bennett not only deals with the emotional side of working in such an extreme medical environment but he also has to be aware of the latest technology and research that is happening to minimise or assist with some of the medical conditions that can make the development and birth of a healthy baby take an unexpected turn. Pregnancy and birth can include unpredictable events that can cause concern for the parents and also the medical staff. If there are ways and means to more accurately monitor conditions or more closely predict the outcome of a particular pregnancy or birth, then Bennett wants to be able to know about it. Research is the medical field that is constantly developing and growing.

'Current research by Professor Colditz looks at assessing foetal movements. There's sometimes a subjective mother's view of "my baby's not moving as much", and this research looks at when that correlates with something actually being wrong. Decreased foetal movement warrants a number of tests and Paul's team is trying to quantify that by using a device that measures movements, the device is called an "accelerometer".

'It is not dissimilar to the technology used in a pedometer where you count how many steps or kilometres you have done during the day. Similar technology monitors how much movement the baby's done during the day, and will [set off an] alarm if there is any diversion from normal and so prompt further investigations. It certainly is a very good idea; the technology is simple and I believe it will work.'

There is also research being conducted into the effects of 'emotional' issues that medical staff face when dealing with the grief and loss that parents experience. This is important to help change the way medical procedures are done or to set up ways of minimising stress on the parents, and on the medical staff.

'Recently there was an undergraduate midwifery course and they were looking at the students who had been on clinical rotations and exposed to significant episodes of grief and loss in their clinical experience. I read one of their big aims was to improve the structure and fashion in which they taught issues on grief and loss to midwifery students and that is equally as important for medical students.

'I am sure that, for most families, the way their midwife deals with them and their experience is one of the biggest factors influencing their healthcare perception. Probably as much if not more than their contact with their doctor, probably more. Mainly because you can expect the midwife will spend ten times as much time with the family.

'One of the most difficult times for a doctor who cares for babies are moments of defeat, when despite one's best efforts a baby passes away. Perhaps [even] more difficult is to arrive at that moment of defeat, evidenced by the futility of ongoing treatment, when a baby remains critical on life supportive measures. Decisions regarding the end of life and withdrawal of treatment are extremely difficult for the doctors who care for babies, and even harder for families when they are faced with such a recommendation from the team who are caring for their baby.'

Di and Marea's story

Di and Marea are registered midwives who have worked in maternity wards for many years. They have seen many births ranging from those with the predictable happy ending through to those that have unexpected complications for either the mother or the baby. Di and Marea relate how things were done over 20 years ago and can see how there have been improvements in the hospital system.

'I [Di] started in 1984. [Back then terminations were done for] fetal abnormalities. Parents didn't get referrals to psychologists and social workers. They didn't get all the things that you get today, like the handprints and the footprints and the nice little teddy or the memorial information. I imagine that the parents did have to organise some sort of burial for the child, but I don't remember what they did.

'In those times, the parents would check out of the hospital without their baby and there was traditionally no support to follow up or see how they were doing. The grieving process for these parents was stalled because the death of their baby wasn't formally acknowledged. The way of coping back then was to "just get on with it". This practice is now not encouraged and there is a more caring approach that is aimed at making a traumatic situation for the family a little less so.

'What they do now is just amazing. No one ever really recognised that a miscarriage might mean the loss of a child to someone, it was never recognised, it was basically a miscarriage and nobody would have thought of it as a child, even though the woman who lost the child probably still remembered. But nobody really thought it was a big deal, that was just life.

'I had a friend who had twins and lost one of them and I said, "This is what we do now, we have all these mementoes, pictures and all this support . . . We give people a lot of support now."

'And she just sat there and started crying. She'd lost this baby to an infection, and whenever there's a birthday or she looks at the twin sister she thinks about the other one. At the time, she'd walked into the nursery and they threw the healthy baby at her, the one that was okay, and said, "We're doing things with the other one." Basically, she never saw her sick baby after that. They just took her away, and she never got to hold her after she'd died; she never got a funeral, she doesn't know where she's buried, she knows absolutely nothing about that child. It was tragic. She had no counselling, no social work involvement, she just left the hospital and took the one baby.'

The practice of providing handprints and footprints is a positive way of helping parents remember their baby. It makes the baby real and creates a memento of their special child, and more importantly, helps the parents grieve properly for their lost child.

'There's barely anybody who doesn't want to take the footprints or handprints home – parents usually do. However, if they don't take them home they have options, they're in their files, so they can get them even if it's 20 years down the track, they can still get these footprints.

'Some people just want to walk away and forget it. Some people don't want to see their baby. They just want to walk out of here and not have anything to do with it. They believe that it was the work of God, and that's that.'

Di and Marea give an insider's view into how people cope with the loss of their child and the longing to find ways to remember their child. In their grief and stress it can be hard to think clearly but Marea and Di always encourage the parents to look at the different options they have to be with their baby.

As Marea has found, 'Some people don't want to see their baby at all. But most do. They might be a little scared of what they're going to see. I had a dad once, and the mother didn't want to see the baby, but he did, so I took him into another room and made a little bath filled with warm water and laid the baby in the bath for him. And he just needed to do that.'

Di relates another experience of grieving parents. Their baby was born and lived for three days. Unfortunately when the baby was born she had major developmental and health complications and the decision was made not to resuscitate her when she stopped breathing. Di did everything she could to help the parents prepare for the loss and honour the memory of their little girl.

'I had this couple, I came in to do the caesarean care and introduced myself. The mum suddenly said to me that there was a toy that was with the baby and she really, really wanted it.

'I said, "I'll go get it and chase it up for you." I got the toy and took it back and quickly said, "Your daughter was just beautiful." And [the mother] just crumbled. It turned out that she hadn't held her baby, I don't even think she'd seen the baby. She asked me if it was too late and I said, "Of course it isn't."

'From that moment, the baby came in and never left her side until they were discharged. They did get to dress her, they got to bathe her, [take] so many photos. The baby actually lived for a few days before she died. I wanted to help the parents create as many memories of this baby alive that I could.

'We did all sorts of things; we filled up the adult bath and we put Mum in the bath with the baby. And we put her in the pram and we ran outside so the sunshine and the daylight were on her skin. It was really great. She was a real baby and I wanted her to experience things rather than staying in hospital in their little depressing four walls, and get outside.

'They looked after their baby for the three days. Very challenging and hard, but at the same time, very rewarding. And the parents will never forget those days. And that's how I get comforted myself. I'll be satisfied with that. Sometimes you look for closure, and in some ways you get it.'

Di and Marea face these sorts of situations nearly every day and it can take its toll on them emotionally. To help get through each difficult time, people in nursing and midwifery band together and debrief to help share stories and support each other.

Di gives her take on how she deals with her emotions and the situations, on how to deal with the grief and the stress felt by the parents.

'It's the same with a perinatal loss. Sometimes you just find yourself standing there crying with the mother, and if you do that, or you're feeling a bit emotional, you can walk into the staff room and there will be someone there who will give you a hug or who will talk to you and sit down with you and have a chat and supervise you even if they are busy. They will still do it. You know, we do support each other pretty well.

'I think nurses, particularly at where I work, are pretty supportive and look after each other. I prefer leaving it at work. I mean if you let it crush your life at home you'll just get emotional about stuff. I just find it's better just to leave it [at work].

'Occasionally, I get a little bit sad, but generally I like to do a good job and look after people and give them as much support as possible. There's no shame in any part of crying. I think it's nice to share your emotional side. Tears come to my eyes every day, but I just got used to it, you know, I feel sad.

'I think that they don't want someone who is cruel and cool and not feeling something. I think they're moved to see that you have a little bit of empathy. I've never lost a child, never been pregnant and never been married, but I can still feel quite a bit of empathy, even though I don't know what it's like to lose a child.'

Marea reiterates Di's sentiments.

'I think that people are quite capable of feeling the loss even if they have had children or not. I always, after looking after a family, walk them out to their car and say goodbye.

'I just happened to be there when this husband said, "Um, what will happen to Heidi when we go?"

'I said, "Well, I'll come and get her and take her down to the mortuary," and he said, "Can I take her down?"

'He carried the baby down from the third floor all the way down the stairs to the mortuary, he didn't want to go in the lift. He said, "I want this to take as long as possible."

'I was walking along beside him. I couldn't fall to bits when he's like that, but when they are gone, that's when I cry.

'I remember saying to my husband one time, "You're just so good, you listen to everything I say when I come home."

'And he said, "I'm not listening sometimes, you know."

'I said, "You look like you are; but that's all I need. I just need an ear."'

Professor Paul Colditz, Professor David de Kretser, AC and Professor Euan Wallace give their views on working in the field of medical research and on the ways they see that the medical profession can head in order to reduce the incidence of stillbirth, miscarriage and neonatal death and increase awareness of infertility issues.

Professor Paul Colditz, MBBS, FRACP, FRCPCH, MBiomedEng, DPhil (Oxford)
Professor of Perinatal Medicine, University of Queensland Royal Brisbane & Women's Hospital

Professor Paul Colditz's inspiring work revolves around human life and in particular giving a better quality of life to sick babies, finding answers through medical research to save more babies, and helping families and indigenous communities so they have the best possible care available to them in these difficult circumstances.

Paul is an exceptional person in the world of perinatal medicine — he is personable, compassionate and gives his time and energy openly.

'SIDS [Sudden Infant Death Syndrome] has been reduced by 80 per cent, there aren't too many things we can knock on the head and reduce by 80 per cent. The rate of SIDS is now half or a third as common as the kind of miscarriage where babies get right through to the last quarter of their gestation and die unexpectedly. If they were to be born alive, they would have every chance of surviving, and if you do the autopsy on these babies then you can't find why they died. Just that group alone, forget about all the earlier pregnancy losses and so on, is much more common than SIDS.

'First of all you have got to have the methods to look at the baby and the methods are very limited and almost solely constrained to ultrasound. Ultrasound is fantastic but there are significant advances like four-dimensional ultrasound . . . now that will give you almost like a photo of your baby in utero, moving across time. But it doesn't necessarily tell you too much about how the baby's going to be in three or four days or weeks; a nice technology but with severe limitations in terms of how you might try to prevent those babies from dying.

'If you talk to mums, there is often the sense that the foetal movements decreased over time, rather than 100 per cent one day. In retrospect there are often feelings that things maybe weren't going so well over days, if not longer.

'The Dutch have led the field in trying to work out what the normal baby does by using ultrasound over longer time periods. If you ask the mum to press a button every time she feels her baby move, she gets it wrong, fairly often. So that's the real problem, you can't necessarily rely on Mum, if you try and incorporate that into clinical practice.

'Randomised control trials have been done and effectively what they showed was that having mums armed with a system where they had to record their fetal movements and if they fall below a particular number, give us a ring . . . we know that did not have an impact on reducing fetal deaths. It left the whole area in limbo. Obstetricians threw away kick charts because the evidence was they don't work. We know that mums' reports of fetal movements and what the baby was actually doing are significantly different things.

'So, we have come up with a technology that can actually measure fetal movement, but in our first phase (there are several phases) it is not going to stop babies from dying tomorrow or even in a year or two. We have to look at higher risk groups initially, to test our hypothesis that the baby will start moving differently – either a reduced amount of movement in quantity or quality – when they become compromised or sick.

'If you look at kids, for instance, you know they're sick because they are quiet and won't get out of bed. So we are sort of thinking the same thing in the baby, they're either going to reduce their quantity or quality of movement and we will be able to get a handle with this simple non-invasive technique to measure foetal movement.

'I think the public's perspective is that it spends a fair bit of money on research, and there are some real breakthroughs that come along – like the new Australian-developed cervical cancer vaccine – and it certainly makes the research investment worthwhile. But where are we going with stillbirth?

'We are not doing really well because of a very misdirected view that some of this is not as important as other directions that the health research dollar might go; somehow there is a concept that it's a baby that never existed, so let's get on with things. Where that misses out, putting things very bluntly, is that not only did an individual die, but that's someone who potentially could have been productive – we apply that standard sort of formula to cancer research, cardiovascular research and so on: if we spend our dollars here and you get a bit of a remission and you live five years longer and some of that is productive, then the economic rationalists will do the cost-benefit analysis and say that it's okay to use this treatment to keep this person alive for a couple of years.

'If you apply that model to stillbirth, then they have got 70 years, and we have got to assume that will be a productive 70 years, so it's an absolute winner in terms of the economic rationalists' model of what the individuals could return back to society. I think if you apply the standard sort of thing as in the broad research area, then stillbirth has got to come up a winner in terms of investing research dollars to try to reduce the number of deaths. And there are real costs, costs of grief and lost productivity in the survivors.

'I think we have got a bit of a blind spot in society, saying, "Well, you know this baby never existed and let's just get on with things and not put that into the statistics," as if that's somehow Nature's way of dealing with something. But we have got statistics about how many of these babies die. I think it probably comes back to really fundamental problems that we all have about thinking and dealing with death.

'It is part of people's mindset saying that, "Well, it is only a miscarriage." I think there are two quite distinct groups. You certainly can't expect good outcomes if there is a severe disorder in the arrangement of the chromosomes early on and this is the cause of a miscarriage. I am not saying that all early miscarriages fit this bill of being severely abnormal fetuses. If you look at the group where everything is fine until quite late in gestation when something goes wrong, we need to do more research basically to find out why that's the case. I think it is a reasonable assumption that those fetuses, if they could be identified and could be taken out of what is a hostile environment, would be entirely normal in the future.

'I suppose that's an example of a research approach where in the cycle of three to five years we could actually make a big difference in a population sense.

'Obviously, science does have some fantastically powerful tools now and they're applied to cancer, they're applied to infectious diseases, they're applied to cardiovascular disease . . . and they can be applied to this whole spectrum of miscarriage. We could apply some of these fantastically powerful tools to try and understand what is actually going on.

'These methods allow us to look at babies who are small because there has been something hostile in their environment, which means they haven't grown to their potential, or the mums who have had a miscarriage and then compare them to a group of women who have gone through and delivered at term and we can apply these tools to say what's different. This is in the whole broader area of molecular biology; it intersects with genetics and uses powerful tools like micro-array techniques. Each of the capital cities in Australia has at least one major research group who have got the capacity to do this kind of research.

'You can then start to work out, is it something like inflammation? Is it something like genetic issues that produce different proteins in the body that is different between these populations? So we can start to back-engineer, if you like, knowing what the differences are. Mums who are at high risk can be identified early and they need high surveillance. One doesn't want to leave the mum 1,000 kilometres from a capital city and think everything's fine, if, for example, she has a high risk of delivering preterm.

'We are starting to scratch the surface and are getting some runs on the board and there are a couple of groups in Australia, and certainly others internationally, who are publishing the papers saying we have identified protein X or gene X, and it has an association with adverse outcomes. It might be high blood pressure in pregnancy, it might be prematurity. Clearly, that's the very exciting step along the way, but it can only be realised by significant investment in research dollars.

'Obviously, what the aim is longer term, is not only to be able to identify these women, but use that knowledge about the cause to start to deal with the root cause. If it's inflammation then why is the inflammation present? Which part of the inflammatory process is involved? [Trying to] block that component, for instance, would be a standard kind of experiment to do. So you can see that if you can identify the risk, there is a chance the woman will get the relevant treatment and the treatment will prevent the outcome.

'That whole powerful kind of new paradigm, molecular biology and genetics, has the potential to make big impacts here. Inflammation of the right degree at the right time, is definitely good, but get it slightly wrong, too much of a degree or slightly the wrong time, then it's bad. Take blood clotting. You've got one system that is designed to clot your blood and you've got one system designed to thin your blood, and we need both of those working in concert. Sometimes we need the blood a bit thinner, sometimes we need it a bit thicker. If we cut ourselves we need it to be a lot thicker around the cut. With haemophilia, you bleed all the time too much. Take it the other way, you clot too much and end up with a DVT [Deep Vein Thrombosis] in an aeroplane. The same with blood sugar control, pretty much any vital system in the body has this balance.

'In our own research we have just started looking at inflammation in the brain after a shortage of oxygen. We know that there can be some very immediate effects and the cells can be dead within hours or days and that's where most of our research is focused to prevent this. If you're a baby trying to develop with inflammation that was caused by the original hypoxia [lack of oxygem], then it may limit the brain's potential to remodel.

'Inflammation is a very complex area, but there is strong evidence that it could be absolutely central to miscarriage, growth restriction, foetal death and cerebral palsy. These inflammatory mediators can get into the brain and they can be either good guys or bad guys. We certainly need more fundamental research around inflammation in pregnancy and there are a number of Australian groups that are making contributions in that area.

'It's a matter of political will, social perception and making the economical rationalist argument.

'We don't need new technologies in a sense, the technology was there five years ago, but there is so much that we could do with the technology that we have available today. We are not waiting for the next technology breakthrough; it's about commitment.

'In a sense, the public does need to understand that there is an element of risk and that the time line isn't immediate, but look at the potentials. It is going to affect a huge number of people and have huge economic impacts.

'Taking our current state of affairs into account, we are pretty good at saving babies if they are born prematurely in the right place and they're big enough, that is from 23 or 24 weeks gestation. But we know that a range of disabilities is over represented in that group compared to a term born group. We have got to remember that term babies are the vast majority of babies, and that the very preterm are only a tiny proportion.

'If you go into any school and you look at those performing in the bottom 10 per cent of kids, it's these who are going to need special support. The vast majority of those were born at preterm. We know the risk of educational low achievement for preterm is very, very much higher, so clearly we ought to be doing something early about trying to prevent this.

'If we look at the smallest babies that have got a good chance of survival, the risk of cerebral palsy might be 10 per cent. It depends how you look at it; if you have been a long time trying to get pregnant and you value the baby very highly, then 10 per cent might be seen as an acceptable risk and of course the cerebral palsy may not be significantly disabling. But if you look at it the other way round, it would be so much better to have the risk much lower than 10 per cent, because there is a lot of anguish and cost engendered by disability.

'In that very tiny group, they have about a 50 per cent risk, versus the term baby with about a 10 per cent risk, of ending up at near the bottom of the class. And whilst those kids, of course, can be loving and responsive and a delight, they're going to have difficulties. They are not going to be able to generate wealth in society in the same way that somebody in the middle of the class can generate it.

'So why is it that their brains are developing in that way? Because, if we can find out why, then we can do something about it and these kids are going to end up alive and in the middle of the class.

'We can do that, but it's got to take the investment to support the research effort.

'What I haven't touched on is the human side, and clearly that is something I am involved in and that is something that touches the heart rather than the hard cold cash side of how society decides to invest its money. So many people are affected so deeply at such a personal level, particularly the mothers. But the fathers are involved as well. We do have to focus back onto how we can make an impact on these very human issues of dealing with grief.

'If we take the example of cancer, it's about trying to stop death and people seem to be able to deal with that much more readily, and they recognise the value of research and are happy to invest in it. With [miscarriage and] stillbirth we need, for exactly the same reason, to make an impact through research. However, as a society we seem to be having more difficulty appreciating the value of such research. I know you will have plenty of stories directly from people who have experienced [miscarriage and] stillbirth and who can express the tragedy from their own hearts.

'It is hard seeing just what goes on in people's hearts.

'You need examples to get through to people. There is much work to be done to develop an appreciation of the mortality that goes on and has far-reaching effects.'

Professor David de Kretser, AC
Governor of Victoria

Professor David de Kretser, AC was born in 1939 in Colombo, Sri Lanka, and migrated to Australia in 1949. He received his Bachelor of Medicine and Bachelor of Surgery degrees from the University of Melbourne in 1962, and his Doctorate of Medicine from Monash University in 1969. His doctoral research focused on the structure and function of the human testis.

Professor de Kretser was the founding Director of the Monash Institute of Reproduction and Development from 1991-2005, (now known as the Monash Institute of Medical Research), and has been a Professor of Anatomy at the Faculty of Medicine of Monash University since 1978. Professor de Kretser's research into reproductive biology, infertility and endocrinology has seen over 600 papers featured in national and international peer-reviewed journals, and over 65 of these papers being presented at international meetings.

From June 1999 to December 2001, Professor David de Kretser served on the Medical Board of the Bonnie Babes Foundation. He was made an Officer of the Order of Australia in 2001, received the Centenary Medal in 2003 and became a Companion of the Order of Australia in 2006 (AC).

Professor de Kretser and his wife Jan have four sons, and five grandchildren. He was named Victorian Father of the Year in 2001. Professor de Kretser assumed office as the twenty-eighth Governor of Victoria on 7 April 2006.

'My research career involved the study of the way in which hormones control various aspects of male reproductive function, ranging from the production of sperm to the actions and production of the hormone testosterone, which is responsible for developing and maintaining the secondary sexual characteristics of men.

'The basic research has had an important outcome of assisting in the management of men with infertility and men who also have problems of low testosterone production.

'In my experience of dealing with men who have infertility, it is also a devastating blow which can cause depression and disturb the relationship between partners. Men tend to internalise their feelings and often have difficulty in feeling free to communicate or show how such a loss has affected them.

'This is particularly important because men confuse their ability to father a child with their virility. This often leads to a reluctance to engage in intimacy with their wife or partner and can cause significant depression.

'One of my family members, to whom I am related by marriage, has experienced the loss of a child during birth and it was a tragic and devastating experience.

'Also, through close links between the Ritchie Centre for Baby Health and the Monash Institute of Medical Research, which I directed, I have met many other families who have lost a baby during pregnancy or in the first year or two of life. The pain and grief that they suffer continue for a considerable length of time and can be quite devastating.

'In my view, the Bonnie Babes Foundation adds a point of contact for those who have experienced the loss of a child in pregnancy or in the early years of life. This point of contact is important in assisting families to deal with the grief of this loss and in guiding such families to appropriate health professionals and other families who have had a similar experience.

'The ability to have a child is important to a large number of couples in society today. This remains an issue despite the fact that many young people today postpone until their childbearing age is well beyond 30.

'This can cause significant difficulties if a problem arises as women's fertility declines in the late 30- and particularly the early 40-year decade. Postponing fertility makes it difficult for a doctor to assist women late in their childbearing age resulting in a greater use of technologies earlier in the infertility management process.'

Professor Euan M Wallace, MBChB, MD, FRCOG, FRANZCOG
Professor of Obstetrics, Monash University

Member of the Bonnie Babes Foundation Medical Board Professor Euan Wallace trained in Edinburgh, completing both his clinical and research training at the Simpson Memorial Maternity Pavilion and the University of Edinburgh's Centre for Reproductive Biology. He came to Australia in 1996 as a Fellow in Maternal-Foetal Medicine, was appointed a Senior Lecturer at Monash University in 1997 and an Associate Professor in Obstetrics in 2001.

In 2006 he was appointed Professor of Obstetrics at Monash University and Director of Obstetric Services for Southern Health (Monash Medical Centre, Dandenong Hospital and Casey Hospital), overseeing Victoria's largest provider of maternity services.

He currently leads a research group in perinatal medicine and is Clinical Director of the Centre for Women's Health Research — the research arm of the Monash University Department of Obstetrics and Gynaecology.

Euan's interest, apart from the medical, is the need for community groups and health professionals to work more closely together to find solutions to help people who experience the loss of their babies and find the reasons why and ways to prevent some of the tragedies that occur during pregnancy and birth. He believes that Australia is leading the way in perinatal research.

'My research and clinical interests are in "all things pregnancy", but particularly in early pregnancy loss, multiple pregnancy, foetal abnormalities, placental development, pre-eclampsia, foetal growth and neuroprotection, and stem cell biology.

'Given our size, Australia is a major contributor to perinatal research and is recognised as one of the leading nations in this area – a great achievement for a small country. There are five or six very active research groups around the country that regularly publish and present their work at major world meetings.

'I think that there are two broad areas of research that are particularly exciting and promising – early pregnancy events and late pregnancy complications.

'In early pregnancy, we are increasingly recognising the importance of the "dialogue" that occurs between the very early baby/placenta and its mother. This dialogue underpins a healthy pregnancy and problems with these events lead to problems across all of pregnancy including miscarriage and later complications. As we understand more about these very early pregnancy events we should be able to improve pregnancy outcomes and reduce complications.

'As for late pregnancy complications, preterm birth and pre-eclampsia remain our major issues, and new developments in cardiovascular medicine may bring new therapies for pre-eclampsia. Managing preterm birth and the preterm infant must remain a major focus of research. Our work is aimed at preventing neurological impairment during the pregnancy so that the eventual outcome of the preterm infant is much better.

'This is very promising as we hope to be able to prevent complications such as cerebral palsy, most of which occurs during the pregnancy rather than at birth or after.

'Our second area that is particularly exciting is the use of stem cells to improve neonatal lung function in the very preterm infant. We have shown that some very special stem cells that we collect from term placenta, not embryos, can be used to repair lung damage. We are now exploring whether the lung damage that happens in the preterm infant can be repaired by these cells. We hope that such therapy in the future may be a major step forward in the clinical care of these tiny infants.'

Chapter 12

The hospital experience

Staff in most hospitals work within the constraints of protocol, and the infrastructure they themselves are a part of. Generally those working at the coalface of the hospital system are incredibly caring and know what is required of them.

There is not a lack of respect or compassion on the part of health professionals as highlighted in recent media reports, but the system in place to deal with miscarriage and stillbirths has its shortcomings.

Adequate training of staff and constant review of systems and protocol is necessary to ensure optimising holistic care for families faced with such a loss. The system is currently undergoing substantial revision, which will lead to a welcomed change.

Confidently approaching the health and hospital system

It is important that you are comfortable with your choice of doctor or healthcare provider. Always ask around for referrals from friends or members of support groups who have had a similar experience regarding pregnancy, miscarriage or premature birth and ask their advice on who they found to be helpful. Of course, if you are a public patient or privately insured, this will also affect your choice of doctors or midwives. Do your own research on the hospitals in your area to get an idea of how you will be treated in an emergency or when the time comes for you to give birth. Compile a list of questions that you can ask your doctor or healthcare provider each time you visit them for a check-up. It is important that you raise any concerns you may have, no matter how small you might think they are, with your medical support team.

Keep in mind that you are entitled to seek a second opinion from another doctor or healthcare provider if you are not comfortable or satisfied with the answers or medical treatment you are receiving. Do not feel that you have to stay with one doctor if they don't seem to match with what you and your partner want in terms of medical treatment.

Seeking appropriate medical treatment

One of the most important decisions you will make once you are ready to fall pregnant or have found out you are pregnant is selecting who you will see for your antenatal care. Your doctor or healthcare provider can offer advice on how you can prepare yourself physically and point you in the right direction if you need some emotional support during your pregnancy. Your treating doctor or healthcare provider is your first point of call and you need to feel confident that they have access to a wide range of services and are up-to-date on current medical information and willing to refer you to specialists if needed or requested.

If you have a particular medical condition or have knowledge of pregnancy or birth complications that may arise, ask your doctor or healthcare provider and the hospital you will be giving birth in how they will cope with emergencies such as miscarriages, premature babies and pregnancy complications. You can also ask questions about your doctor or healthcare provider's availability, such as will they be willing to take non-emergency calls if you have a question, will they see you for all your antenatal check-ups, are they affiliated with a major hospital that has a neonatal intensive care unit and will they be available for the birth and able to deal with a preterm delivery.

Lucy Turnbull

Lucy Turnbull, the former Lord Mayor of Sydney and wife of the Federal Opposition Leader, Malcolm Turnbull, believes that the healthcare system is dealing at its full potential with these specific areas of pregnancy loss.

'The condition of the health care system, like the hospital system itself, is a fairly blunt instrument to deal with miscarriage and pregnancy loss and not just because of lack of resources and lack of the way things are organised. I feel it would be a very positive step if people who are experiencing pregnancy loss or stillbirth were placed in an area which doesn't constantly remind them of the child that they have lost, or the premature or unwell child that is struggling in intensive care – wherever that is possible.

'Like a difficult birth event, like having a premature child or a child in intensive care, it is hard to reconcile this with lying in an obstetric ward with other gurgling babies their mothers and their happy families surrounding you. Of course you have just had a child, and, on one level you are rightly there just like the other mothers of newborns. And you are very happy for the other mums and their healthy babies. But on the other hand, not having your baby there to nurture and cuddle like the other mums is very sad especially when people are constantly asking you where your baby is and what has happened.

'I think it is very important to have time to build yourself back up and get help. Organisations like Bonnie Babes (and these days, access to the internet and the helpful information it can provide) are important parts of the recovery process.'

A midwife's story

Amanda is a midwife at an outer suburban hospital in Victoria and she has been instrumental in the ways the hospital deals with pregnancy loss. Many people see it as more progressive in dealing with the issues of pregnancy loss. Amanda recounts her experiences in both her professional and personal life.

'Wanting to have babies was a fairly big thing for me, and having miscarriage after miscarriage was disappointing. I have a fairly good perspective on how other people feel when they don't get to have children at all. How it feels to have your dreams shattered. Thinking, *What do I do with the rest of my life?*

'I remember the first one, we were both really still young and the father cried.

'I think it was probably sadder for me, after five of them, I did a bit of sorting out. I spent quite a few days away with a lot of other women in a retreat, we did a ceremony to honour our babies who died. Some of their beliefs were a bit different, but getting to deal with things was good. It made me realise there were lots of different sorts of grief.

'Not having children can be as big or as small as other grief, like people who lose husbands because of their divorce, or a house has burnt down – it's all relative and you have to learn to move on eventually.

'The reason I became a midwife was because my sister had a termination for abnormalities, and I was with her during that. They brought the baby to her in a kidney dish and I thought, *No! This can be done better*.

'Now, I'm a Pregnancy Loss Coordinator. If there is a foetal death or someone has an abnormality and has chosen to have a termination, the doctors liaise with me and I ring the parents and ask if they would like to come and see me so we can talk about what has happened, and what to expect when they come into hospital. I show them, if possible, the room they will be in, tell them who will look after them, and briefly mention a few things to do with support groups etc, so they know where to get help.

'After they go home they are followed up by me and the social worker, usually about two weeks after, because that's when they are trying to get back into normal activity, then again at six weeks, and then after that whenever they want to, then on the anniversary date the next year.

'We have packages made up in take-home bags, with information on grief, where to contact support groups or counselling, Bonnie Babes being one of the contacts. The bag also includes all their mementoes, photos, foot and handprints, clothing and blankets. I try to make sure that things are done properly. That information is clear and understood.

'This job is very satisfying, challenging, sad and beautiful. But also, people do come back and have healthy babies, so that makes it a joy as well.'

Knowledge is also power, so it is important that you understand what might occur during pregnancy, birth and post-delivery, which will also help you frame your own questions relevant to your individual health and medical needs. Explore all the options available to you and your baby in relation to doctors and specialists, midwives and registered nurses, public and private hospitals and facilities that are easily accessible and available.

Chapter 13

Creating memories – a summary

Establishing rituals for remembrance

When a baby dies, most people's first reaction is to ask, 'Why?' It seems so pointless. Just as life has begun, it has ended. Those who are religious may wonder why the child was given and then taken away so quickly. The mother may ask herself, 'Why did this happen to us, did we do something wrong?' The mother may also ask herself if she did the right things during the pregnancy or if she could have somehow prevented the death.

The death of a baby brings about a confusing and painful time for many people and it can be difficult to decide what should be done when all the family members are grieving in their different ways. Often the most painful part is that they were not given the chance to really know the baby, that there are few memories to cling to during their grief.

Something to remember

One way to help a family through the grief of losing a baby is to create special memories of the child. Your funeral director can help with this process and assist you in coming to terms with what has happened and in recognising the life of the baby, however short it may have been.

Naming the child

Sometimes it can be easier to speak about the death if the child has been given a name. This also helps in recognising that although life may have been short, it was a life nonetheless and should be acknowledged as such. For those who are religious, many religions will allow for a member of their clergy to baptise or christen the child. For those who are not particularly religious, your funeral director can assist with finding a civil celebrant who will be able to perform a naming ceremony. Some funeral directors will be able to present you with a naming certificate. Alternatively, you may like to organise a family gathering to informally name the baby and pay tribute to their life.

The importance of a funeral

A funeral of the baby can be of great assistance in helping the family through the grief process. The funeral service provides a chance for the family to share their pain and support each other in their grief. It also provides recognition of the baby's life, just as naming does.

Some hospitals may suggest that they arrange an unattended burial. Do not make any decisions of this kind straightaway. You will have a couple of days to think about any ceremonies you would like for the baby. It is better to take your time to decide what you really want than always to remember the death with the added burden of regret that you didn't say goodbye in a manner you would have liked.

Family members may also make arrangements without consulting the parents to 'take the weight from their shoulders'. However, making decisions about the funeral arrangements can aid the parents in coming to grips with the difficult fact that their baby has died. While family help should never be belittled, the loss is primarily that of the parents and they need to be able to decide how they wish to handle it.

Elements of a baby's funeral

What should be included in a funeral service for a baby? Once again, this is the parents' decision. Many options are possible.

- The funeral can be held in a funeral home, at a church, at the gravesite or even a family member's home. It should be wherever you feel most comfortable.
- Photographs of the baby may be of comfort in years to come to help families in remembering.
- The option of burial or cremation is still open (and the ashes can be distributed in various ways), whichever feels the most appropriate.
- A memorial book with the signatures and perhaps photographs of those who attended the funeral can be made.
- Some family members might like to hold the baby in their arms. A funeral director can arrange a viewing to allow this to take place.

The family's grief

Members of the family may grieve in different ways and for different reasons at the death of a baby. Grandparents regret the loss of the grandchild they were looking forward to holding and may ask, 'Why couldn't it have been me instead?' They also ache for their own children, seeing them in pain and powerless to ease this pain. Siblings, particularly those who may have felt that the new baby took their parents' attention away, may think the death was their fault. Parents can feel that they did something wrong to deserve this terrible loss.

Each family member should play their part in this support network and help each other to rise above the grief without forgetting for a moment that a very important life has ended.

Creating memories

For many parents and families, spending time with the baby and creating as many memories as possible honours the baby's life and existence. Creating memories and then sharing them over time is a real key to healing for many parents who have experienced the death of their baby. These special times, ceremonies and rituals can provide much comfort. Some other ways of creating memories include:

- Putting together a baby album that includes photographs, ultrasounds, a lock of hair, an identity bracelet, footprints and handprints, records of weight, include anything that reminds you of your pregnancy and the time spent with your baby.
- Writing a letter, song or poem to or about the baby.
- Preparing a family tree including the baby.
- Keeping a journal recording thoughts and feelings about the baby.

- Holding a memorial service or blessing on anniversaries or birthdays.
- Planting a tree of remembrance, perhaps one that flowers around the anniversary of your baby's birth.
- Designing a memorial to place on the baby's grave or in another special place.
- Making a cross-stitch birth sampler, a photo frame, a memory box, a ceramic tile.
- Adopting a star – see www.starregistry.com.
- Giving gifts to other children during the year to honour your baby.

Anniversaries can be a difficult time and throughout the years these particular times will be painful. There are a number of ways to acknowledge these special times. You can:

- Make a donation to a favourite charity in your baby's name.
- Donate flowers to a hospital, church or temple.
- Hold a memorial service.
- Light a candle.

Always do whatever feels right for you and your partner to help remember your baby. Finding ways to remember your baby is important for your grieving process and to remind yourself that you are a parent who has had a child.

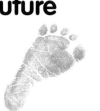

Chapter 14

The future

Falling pregnant again

As you contemplate the possibility of becoming pregnant again, you may find that your feelings fluctuate from one day to the next, even from one moment to the next. Sometimes you may think that all you want to do is get pregnant again, while at other times you can't bear the thought of going through the potential heartache. This feeling of uncertainty is a natural thing and perfectly normal for any woman who has suffered a pregnancy loss. To add to your confusion, you will no doubt have friends and family giving you many different opinions on what you should do and how long you should wait before falling pregnant. Ultimately it is your and your partner's decision based on how you both feel about trying for another pregnancy. It is a journey that you will make together, bravely facing whatever outcome that pregnancy will bring.

Physical readiness

You will need to be sure that you are physically ready to handle another pregnancy. If you are concerned about your physical readiness consult with your doctor or healthcare provider. If you experienced complications in your previous pregnancy or birth, it might be worth looking at possible ways to minimise any risk or discuss any potential of future risk with your doctor.

You might want to prepare your body so that it is healthy and ready for the next pregnancy. For example, you might want to lose extra baby weight or get back into your pre-pregnancy exercise and activities to improve your fitness levels. You may also want to start taking supplements, such as folic acid, to prepare for conception and to give your baby the best possible chance of survival.

There are also a number of factors that will influence your decision to fall pregnant again, either sooner or later, such as your age, the spacing between a brother or sister, fertility problems, health considerations and the strength of your relationship with your partner.

Emotional considerations

As you prepare yourself physically for another pregnancy, you need to consider your emotional readiness. You will have realised that you will never completely forget your pregnancy loss, even though the intensity of the pain that is felt will lessen over time and you come to terms with your loss. If you are still suffering deeply or feel you are in the early stages of grief, it is probably not the most ideal time to prepare for a pregnancy. There is always the possibility that falling pregnant before dealing with your grief adequately can put the grief on hold until after the next baby is born – and the grief may return or you may have unrealistic expectations of the pregnancy and the next born child.

Naturally there is always the fear that what has happened to the previous baby might happen again. It is important to work through this fear on a physical level (by discussing the possibility of a similar condition occurring) and to also face this fear yourself.

A future without a child

Sometimes, despite all the hoping and trying, couples are faced with a different view of their future – a future without children. Whatever the path taken, couples do come to a point during unsuccessful infertility treatment or after experiencing multiple losses that the final outcome is not what they had expected. There are still a number of ways to create a family through adoption or surrogacy or couples may decide to re-examine their expectations and dreams for the future without having children. The most important way of dealing with this decision is as a couple and making communication as open and honest as possible. New hopes and plans for the future will at times be confronting and will bring back the grief of the loss of a baby. Always do what you feel is right for you and your partner.

Of course, there is a choice to make the decision to not have children. This decision brings with it unexpected advantages such as more time to spend on personal hobbies and interests, the time and energy to nurture relationships and the potential to pursue a career without considering parental obligations and responsibilities.

It can take a while, if not a lifetime, to come to terms with the idea of living without children, especially if it has been an important dream. There will be a number of questions that can be addressed by both you and your partner to help clarify how you feel about not having children. Look at the reasons why you wanted to have children. Did you imagine not having children? What can you do to adapt to circumstances and live a fulfilling life together? What can you do together as a couple to explore other joint ambitions or dreams for the future? Find out how you can share your story with others, such as seeking help from a counsellor, joining support groups relevant chat rooms and getting together with couples in similar situations.

You are not alone

Where one person feels heartache and the experience of the loss of a baby, there are others who have similar stories to tell and to share. *Small Miracles* is about support and not suffering in silence, it is about reaching out to others to help you reach out for yourself to find renewed hope and overcome the experience of extreme tragedy. Reaching out and talking about personal experiences, as the stories included here have done, is essential for emotional healing and to help find the courage to be able to look at life from many different perspectives, sometimes in ways that you might never have expected.

It is important to share our stories, to get help when it is needed and to look to the future to keep the circle of life and living complete. Hearing other people's stories also patterns our own journeys – it is this that makes us feel that we are all part of something much bigger than our own private worlds.

Ann was almost three months pregnant when she lost her baby, but she instinctively knew the baby was a girl and chose the name Louise. Over 36 years later Ann says, 'We never stop being a mum.' *Ann Stanton*

I know that being mother of Madison took me on a journey through some aspects of love . . . the strength of mother love . . . the pain of loss . . . and the courage to mother again.

Carol

You know the tears that flood your eyes as you face the unexplainable, 'Why me, why didn't this work?' I mean, that's life, it's a journey of joy and sadness and somehow we all have to learn to cope with that and move on.

Lexy Hamilton-Smith

Many people think miscarriage is 'a sad issue', so it's swept under the carpet . . . It's actually an integral part of the whole process for some women; the whole journey of becoming a parent.

Mara

You do feel like you're the only one at the time; when you do get over that initial grieving time it's good to know there are people out there who you can talk to and understand . . . It's recognition that you have gone through something quite terrible . . .

Clare

As I reflect on my life, the ache is always present. My babies have helped me to come to terms with the knowledge that life is suffering and we must value every moment we have.

Janine

Continuing the journey

Life is fragile. It is not perfect and it can seem, at times, to be filled with sadness and suffering. Many of the couples who have contributed to *Small Miracles* have shown how life can take a dramatic swing from hope to despair, that life is a rollercoaster ride of emotions and unpredictable events. *Small Miracles* hopes to make a contribution to the community understanding the loss of a baby – there is so much more to be said and could have been said, but this book is a starting point for people to look at their own stories and journeys to help them begin to rebuild their lives and learn to embrace the future, whatever it may hold.

Having a miscarriage ourselves at four months gives us first-hand experience in what couples feel with a miscarriage or the loss of a baby. This was in the 80's and there was no counselling foundation like Bonnie Babes to help us to cope with our grief. This is why the Bonnie Babes Foundation is so close to our hearts as working with them we see what a marvellous job they do in helping couples with grief counselling.

Michael and Barbara Warshall

From the time I was a little girl all I wanted to be when I grew up was a mother. Being a mother is the most rewarding job, so when I lost my babies – five miscarriages and one stillborn little boy – it was a very sad and empty feeling . . . I did eventually become a mother and my daughter's name is Ami. I didn't give up, so when I hear the word 'Mummy' I smile.

Sue Wilson

Every beep or alarm made my heart drop inside my chest. They were so small, my little triplet girls. Wires and feeding tubes, round-the-clock nurses; I have never felt so useless. All I could do as a dad was to be there. 'Well, that's pretty much the greatest thing I've ever done in my life!' was what I said moments after I had my first cuddle with one of my little triplet girls.

Eric Stephens

I did get that counselling eventually, but to this day – more than five years later – I still can't talk about my loss without welling up with tears. And I've discovered that I'm not alone. Losing a baby is something that you never quite get over. It's a subject which is not talked about openly, but if it were there would be few women of childbearing age who could honestly say that they had not been affected by the loss of a baby; if not them personally, a sister, relative or a friend who endured pregnancy loss has likely sought their support and comfort.

Toni Ruhle

With my own miscarriages, you think your good friends are the ones supporting you, but people come out of the woodwork. Women are probably good that way that they can bring things into the open and have a good talk about things.

Clare

Despite the heartache of what was to come, we were comforted by the compassion of the doctors who cared for and supported us. The doctor who delivered the diagnosis was kind and beautiful to us. There were so many things that made a difference in those days before delivering Alex. Most of all was the kind and compassionate care of those around us.

Gavin and Kelly

I believe we all have a choice with what we do in the wake of tragedy. My choice was to go on and embrace life fully as the new me. I will never be the person I was before Joseph lived and died, but I can be the new me with that loss incorporated as part of my very being.'

Janine

Some people don't recognise a miscarriage at 14 weeks as being an actual child. But believe me, when you have felt the sickness, or the movement of that life inside of you, that's something between you and your husband; that is something you definitely have to deal with in order to move on and have another healthy pregnancy.

Robert and Danielle Harvey

Not having children can be as big or as small as other grief, like people who lose husbands because of their divorce, or a house has burnt down — it's all relative and you have to learn to move on eventually.

Amanda, a midwife

The fragility of life and death; there's something about walking into a children's hospital, a children's ward, and to see and feel this kind of helplessness that you can't do something for them. It's a kind of consuming feeling when the child is healthy and cries. With little premmie babies, your heart goes out to mothers and fathers that have children that haven't gone full-term, that have to cope with problems.

Tony Bonner

It is important to effectively assist families through their distress and to help them understand that their 'normal' life has changed as they reflect on their loss and adapt to their new circumstances. Families are sensitively reminded that moving through their grief, or trying for another baby, does not mean forgetting or abandoning their loved one. I am always touched by the many beautiful and heartfelt ways families have chosen to remember and celebrate special days, anniversaries or the bonding of the short life of this much-loved lost baby.

Judith Krause

Whispers
A silent breath
A silent smile
Your heart did beat just for awhile
Never forgotten
Sad in grief
Never did your little voice speak
In memory of love
Two souls become one
That's when God had said
Thy will be done.

Jaclyn Rose, mother of two children and four grandchildren, a mum who lost eight babies

Epilogue

Small Miracles is in remembrance of all the babies in the world who have died too soon. And in remembrance of all the premature babies who bravely fight to survive.

It's also to remember, every single day around the world, the dedicated health professionals who care for infants in intensive care units with love and compassion.

Small Miracles is for all the parents who wake up one day and find themselves the guardians of sick babies or whose babies lose the battle to survive.

And personally, for my two sons Joshua and Ezra, who never had the chance to experience life with their dad and me, and my two beautiful healthy boys Daniel-Leigh and Joel, who inspire us every day to find answers, decrease statistics, help families with counselling and continue to supply vital medical equipment.

Remember there is hope for the future, through awareness and education, that the next generation and those that follow will hear their babies cry — and not endure silent tears.

Glossary of medical terms

Antenatal depression

Antenatal depression is depression that starts during pregnancy and lasts more than two weeks. It affects up to 15 per cent of pregnant women and nearly half of those will go on to have postnatal depression.

Congenital abnormalities

The term congenital abnormality refers to any aberration that occurs during foetal development. Any of the major organs, such as the brain, heart, lungs, kidney and limbs may be involved. The severity of these aberrations may range from cosmetic anomalies to life-threatening conditions.

About 2–3 per cent of all babies have what is called a major physical anomaly. This is something that either impacts on the way certain things look, or how they work.

Birth defects involving the brain are the most common problems. They concern about 10 per 1,000 live births, compared to heart problems, at 8 per 1,000, kidney problems at 4 per 1000, and limbs at 1 per 1,000. All other physical anomalies together occur in 6 per 1,000 live births.

Birth defects of the heart have the highest risk of death during childhood. They are the cause of 28 per cent of infant deaths due to birth defects, while chromosomal abnormalities and respiratory abnormalities each account for 15 per cent. About 10 per cent of deaths in children are because of a genetic disease.

Many congenital anomalies can be diagnosed before birth and there is a wide variety of treatment options available depending on the type and severity of the anomaly.

Ectopic pregnancy

During ovulation, an egg (ovum) is released from one of the ovaries. Conception occurs when the egg is met by a sperm in the fallopian tube. Normally, the fertilised egg travels down the fallopian tube and into the uterus, where it buries into the plump uterine lining. Ectopic pregnancy refers to a pregnancy that develops outside of the uterus, most commonly in one of the fallopian tubes that leads from each ovary. In almost all cases, the embryo dies. The developing placenta can't access a rich blood supply and the fallopian tube is not large enough to accommodate the growing embryo. Unfortunately, ectopic pregnancies pose a threat to the mother's life. In one out of five cases, the tube ruptures, causing internal bleeding and shock. This is a medical emergency requiring immediate surgery and blood transfusion.

Over 95 per cent of all ectopic pregnancies are in the fallopian tubes. They can also occur in other sites, such as the cervix (neck of the uterus), the abdominal cavity and the ovary itself. Around two per cent of all pregnancies are ectopic.

Infertility

Primarily refers to the biological inability of a man or a woman or a couple to create a baby. Infertility may also refer to the state of a woman who is unable to carry a pregnancy to full-term. There are many biological causes of infertility, some of which may be bypassed with medical intervention.

In utero

Is another way of referring to 'in the uterus'.

In-Vitro Fertilisation (IVF) and Assisted Reproductive Technology (ART)

In-Vitro Fertilisation is a process where the egg cells are fertilised by the sperm cells outside of the womb, and then implanted into the mother's uterus, typically 3–5 days after fertilisation in a culture. Assisted Reproductive Technology refers to not only IVF but other fertility procedures used to help infertile couples become pregnant. These include fertility medications, sperm injection and donor egg therapy. The treatment will depend on the specific needs of the couple.

Miscarriage

Spontaneous miscarriage is defined as the loss of a pregnancy before 20 weeks gestation. Most spontaneous miscarriages (75 to 80 per cent) occur in the first 12 weeks of pregnancy. It is estimated that one in four pregnancies end in a loss. Many miscarriages are unreported or go unrecognised because they occur very early in the pregnancy, prior to a missed period. Of those who recognise they are pregnant (i.e. after they have missed a period), the risk of miscarriage is around 9–15 per cent.

Neonatal

Pertaining to the period immediately after birth and the first four weeks of life.

Perinatal

According to the World Health Organisation, perinatal defines the period occurring around the time of birth (5 months before and 1 month after). The perinatal period commences at 22 completed weeks (154 days) of gestation (the time when birth weight is normally 500 grams), and ends seven completed days after birth. Other organisations use different criteria.

Placenta praevia

During pregnancy, the placenta provides the growing baby with oxygen and nutrients from the mother's bloodstream. Placenta praevia means the placenta has implanted at the bottom of the uterus, over the cervix or close by.

When a baby is ready to be born, the cervix (neck of the womb) dilates (opens) to allow the baby to move out of the uterus and into the vagina. When a woman has placenta praevia, the baby can't be born vaginally. 'Partial placenta praevia' means the cervix is partly blocked, while 'complete placenta praevia' means the entire cervix is obstructed. Unfortunately, even having a partial placenta praevia may mean it is unlikely the baby can be born vaginally. Some of the causes include scarring of the uterine lining (endometrium) and abnormalities of the placenta. Around one in every 200 pregnancies is affected.

Pre-eclampsia

Pre-eclampsia is a serious disorder of pregnancy characterised by high maternal blood pressure, protein in the urine and severe fluid retention. It is quite common, affecting around five to 10 per cent of all pregnancies in Australia. One to two per cent of cases are severe enough to threaten the lives of both the mother and her unborn child.

Pre-eclampsia accounts for one in five inductions and one in six caesarean sections. The mechanisms behind the condition are mysterious, but genetic factors and the placenta seem to play significant roles. For reasons unknown, pre-eclampsia tends to be more common in first rather than subsequent pregnancies. The mother's blood pressure usually returns to normal as soon as the baby is delivered.

Premature babies

Around 7 per cent of Australian babies are born prematurely (before 37 weeks gestation) every year. The rate is much higher in the United States, at 12 per cent of births. Some babies die as a result of being born too early, but risks are related to the gestation (time spent in the womb) at delivery and birth weight. Those babies who survive often face complications because their organs are too immature to function properly outside the womb. Luckily, the technology available to neonatal intensive care units is so sophisticated that even very preterm babies now have decent survival prospects. A baby born after 30 weeks of gestation can now expect survival to be over 90 per cent. Babies born after 34 weeks of gestation have an excellent outlook.

We know of a few risk factors, but the mechanics behind premature labour remain a mystery. It is difficult to prevent premature labour without fully understanding the reasons for it.

Postnatal depression
Is a form of clinical depression that can affect women, and less frequently men, after childbirth. It is widely considered to be treatable.

Stillbirth
Occurs when a fetus dies in the uterus or during labour or delivery after 20 weeks gestation. The term is often used in distinction to live birth or miscarriage. Most stillbirths occur in full-term pregnancies. Some sources reserve the term 'stillbirth' for a fetus which has died after reaching mid-second trimester to full-term gestational age.

About the Bonnie Babes Foundation

The Bonnie Babes Foundation helps parents come to terms with their loss. The charity helps over 17,000 families each year. The Bonnie Babes Foundation has 24-hour, 7-day per week grief counselling services for those with infertility issues or those who have lost a baby through miscarriage, stillbirth, neonatal loss or prematurity, and the charity raises funds for vital medical research to change the sad statistic of one in every four pregnancies ending in a loss. The charity also purchases important medical equipment for hospitals across Australia to help tiny premmie babies struggling for life. Since its inception the charity has helped to save thousands of babies' lives.

A non-profit volunteer-based charity, the Bonnie Babes Foundation relies on the generosity and compassionate support of the public and caring sponsors.

The charity is not government funded and it is the only organisation of its type in Australia fulfilling all the areas of pregnancy care prior to conception and thereafter. All the services the charity provides for grieving parents and for the birth of healthier babies are free to the public.

To continue its wonderful work the Bonnie Babes Foundation needs more support to enable more precious Aussie babies to survive and live healthier lives.

Our Services

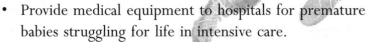

- Provide medical equipment to hospitals for premature babies struggling for life in intensive care.
- Assist vital medical research projects into pregnancy loss and complications to women's health during and following pregnancy.
- Provide education and training for health professionals.
- Provide health, nutrition and wellness advice for women prior to and during pregnancy.
- Provide support for families with infertility issues and assists with counselling relating to infertility.
- Provide support for babies born with congenital malformations.
- Support women who develop pre-eclampsia and other medical conditions during pregnancy.
- Provide extensive public awareness and education about pregnancy loss, infertility issues and prematurely born babies.

The Prime Minister Kevin Rudd has stated: 'The Government congratulates Bonnie Babes Foundation for the significant contribution they provide for families affected by the loss of a baby through miscarriage, through stillbirth or through premature death and related issues such as infertility. They do a very good job. The Government also congratulates them for their contribution to providing medical equipment for the care of premature babies and their support for research.'

The charity is the leader in Australia in pregnancy loss issues and it is the only children's charity dedicated to pregnancy loss issues.

The Bonnie Babes Foundation is partly responsible for initiating the Government's Maternity Services Review and Rachel was invited to participate in forums. The Bonnie Babes Foundation only exists due to public support so it's the kind support from you in purchasing this book or joining the charity as a member that allows the Bonnie Babes Foundation to continue our vital community work. We sincerely thank you.

Professor Paul Colditz

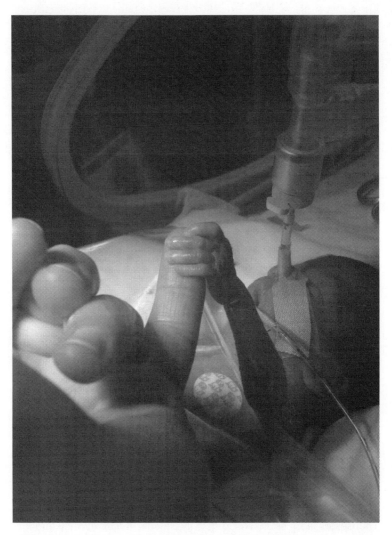

Baby Aria was born at 21.6 weeks and stayed in the NICU for 6.5 weeks.

Grief counselling

When you need to talk to someone . . .

The Bonnie Babes Foundation provides Australia wide, 24-hour 7-day per week free grief counselling services to families who have lost a baby. The Foundation's trained counsellors will provide grief counselling for any member of the family or friends grieving after pregnancy loss. Our counselling services also support families with infertility issues and families who have a baby with an illness or complication following birth. If you would like to organise to speak with one of the Foundation's counsellors, find out more about our community support groups or request any of our free literature on coping with pregnancy loss, please contact us.

Join our caring team of dedicated counsellors . . .

The Foundation's grief counselling services are provided by professionally trained and caring individuals. People from all walks of life complete the course as well as health professionals, psychologists and social workers. There are no prerequisites for participating in the counselling course which is conducted around Australia for individuals who wish to become grief counsellors. The Bonnie Babes Foundation grief counselling course is used across the world; our Grief Counselling Certificate training for peer support counsellors is highly acclaimed in medical circles. Grief counsellors learn strategies to help individuals in their journey through the grief process and the course equips peer support counsellors with the ability to listen to and validate effectively the grief of an individual with infertility issues or experiencing a pregnancy loss through miscarriage, stillbirth or premature birth.

Phone: (03) 9803 1800 or 1300 266 643
Facsimile: (03) 9803 2699
Email: enquiry@bbf.org.au
www.bbf.org.au

The Bonnie Babes Foundation relies on the continued support and encouragement of a number of Ambassadors and Supporters. The Foundation is also ably assisted by the Bonnie Babes Foundation Medical Board.

Special thanks to Bonnie Babes Foundation Psychologist – Betty Chetcuti, BBSc (Hons), MEdPsych, MAPS
Bonnie Babes Foundation Grief Counsellor Trainer and Grief Counsellor – Judith Krause

Patrons and Ambassadors

Glenn Archer	Robert Harvey
Jo Silvagni (Bailey)	Frank Holden
Natarsha Belling	Judy Hopgood
Rachel Berger	Kimberley Joseph
Tony Bonner	Kamahl
Sir Jack Brabham	Paul Kelly
Nathan Bracken	Dale Kickett
Carina Brown	Dr Rosie King
Sally Browne	Steve Leibmann
Richard Champion	Joanna Lockwood
Nicola Charles	Craig Lowndes
Deborah Claxton	Collette Mann
Brett Climo	Glenn Manton
Chantal Contouri	Tom Moody
Alyssa-Jane Cook	Jenny Morris, OAM
Marina Craig	Ronn Moss ('The Bold and The Beautiful')
Lochie Daddo	Patti Newton
John Deeks	Dr Cindy Pan
Lorrae Desmond	Ann Peacock
Denise Drysdale	Diana Plater
Paula Duncan	Glenn Ridge
Diane Dunleavy	Naomi Robson
Judith Durham	Janine Shepherd
Heather Foord	Judy Stone
Belinda Giblin	Deborah Thomas (*The Women's Weekly*)
Rebecca Gibney	Andrew Vlahov
Karla Gilbert	Kathy Watt
Sandy Gore	Stig Wemyss
Jo Hall	The Wiggles
Lexy Hamilton-Smith	Cameron Williams
Danielle Harvey	John Wood

The Medical Board

Bonnie Babes Medical Board consists of the most highly respected perinatal specialists in Australia.

Professor Lesley Barclay – Professor and Director, Northern Rivers University, Department of Rural Health (NSW)

Associate Professor Fiona Bogossian – University of Queensland

Dr Lucy Bowyer – Sub-Specialist, Maternal Fetal Medicine, Royal Hospital for Women (NSW)

Associate Professor Leonie Callaway – Head, Royal Brisbane Clinical School, Staff Specialist, Internal and Obstetric Medicine, Royal Brisbane & Women's Hospital.

Professor Paul Colditz – Director Perinatal Research Centre, Royal Brisbane & Women's Hospital

Dr John Drew – Paediatrician

Professor Warwick Giles – Senior Staff Specialist and Director, Maternal Fetal Medicine, Royal North Shore Hospital

Associate Professor Rajat Gyaneshwar, Clinical Director of Obstetrics and Gynaecology, Liverpool Hospital, (NSW)

Associate Professor Roger Hart – Specialist, Reproductive Medicine and Surgery, Fertility Specialists of Western Australia

Associate Professor Ross Haslam – Head, Neonatal Medicine, Women's & Children's Hospital (SA)

Associate Professor Rosemary Horne, NHMRC Research Fellow, Scientific Director of the Ritchie Centre, Monash Institute of Medical Research

Dr Len Kliman – Epworth Freemasons Hospital, Melbourne

Professor Ian Macreadie – CSIRO Molecular and Health Technologies (Vic)

Leah Magliano – Hobart Private Hospital

Professor Helen McCutcheon – Head, School of Nursing and Midwifery (SA)

Dr Peter McDougall – Chief of Medicine, Director of Department of Neonatology, Royal Children's Hospital

Ms Meredith McIntyre – Monash University, Senior Lecturer, School of Nursing and Midwifery

Associate Professor Lisa McKenna – Monash University, Senior Lecturer, School of Nursing and Midwifery

Dr Karen Mizia – Ultrasound Care

Professor Jeremy Oats – Director of Gynaecology and CPIU, Royal Women's Hospital (Vic)

Dr C. Andrew Ramsden – Director, Newborn Services, Monash Medical Centre

Professor Karen Simmer – Professor, Newborn Medicine, University of Western Australia

Dr Anne Sneddon – Director, Obstetrics and Gynaecology, Canberra Hospital

Dr Brendan Steele – Head, Obstetrics and Gynaecology, Sandringham & District Memorial Hospital

Dr Christine Tippett – Director, Maternal Fetal Medicine Unit, Monash Medical Centre

Dr Stephen Tong – Clinician and Research Scientist, Monash Institute of Medical Research, Monash University

Professor Brian Trudinger – Obstetrics and Gynaecology, Westmead Hospital (NSW)

Professor Euan Wallace – Clinical Director, Centre for Women's Health Research, Monash Institute of Medical Research

Ambassadors and Supporters of Perinatal Medicine Research and Grief Counselling

Tony Bonner's story

Veteran actor Tony Bonner, has given a great deal of his time to help this cause, including hosting a Bonnie Babes Foundation documentary in 1999. Tony is also a Patron of the Bonnie Babes Foundation.

'I know it's a cliché, our futures really revolve around the children of the world and how we treat them and how we teach them. With Bonnie Babes it was a similar thing that anything I could do with a family, fundraising to assist, research, to help families.

'The fragility of life and death; there's something about walking into a children's hospital, a children's ward, and to see and feel this kind of helplessness that you can't do something for them.

'It's a kind of consuming feeling when the child is healthy and cries. With little premmie babies, your heart goes out to mothers and fathers that have children that haven't gone full-term, that have to cope with problems.

'You know it isn't a subject people would readily talk about in the seventies. No one really asked any questions, you just accepted what had happened and didn't speak about it. It was a kind of denial. I'm a great advocate for the system of mentors, people being able to speak what their feelings are. These days, the slight about going to see a psychiatrist or a psychologist is no longer something; I mean, for too many years in England and Australia we didn't ask for help, we didn't process the pain.

'I suppose we didn't understand it and therefore people shut down. It's wonderful to have someone's hand to hold, that's all I've ever done; if I can hold someone's hand, just help them share a bit of a rocky spot in life. No words are really needed for that connection.

'The hand I talk about holding is the hand that Bonnie Babes offers to couples who have lost their precious child before it had a chance in this life. The help offered by Bonnie Babes is what drew me to them.'

Heather Foord's story

Heather Foord has been Brisbane's Network Nine's newsreader for the past decade. Heather hasn't experienced miscarriages or birth complications but her connection to a number of her friends experiencing these has made her passionately involved in raising community awareness. Closer to home, Heather's mother lost a baby and her sister's child was born with complications. Heather is also a Patron of the Bonnie Babes Foundation.

'The problem is that most people say [about miscarriages or the loss of a baby], "Oh well, plenty more, never mind, it wasn't fully formed" – all those really heartless things.

I know what it's like to be pregnant. From that very first moment to me it was this person, this life and every day is an eternity when you are pregnant. I can vaguely understand what women who lose babies must feel like because they are little people and personalities inside you; especially, the more pregnancies you have, you realise how different they all are. It is just very special to the mother.

'[Loss and grief] has always been a taboo subject. When I was little, I went to church and all the old ladies there had these tiny little woollen jackets that they had knitted, and being a child I thought they were toy clothes, baby doll dresses and the women explained, "Oh darling, these are for the little babies that died in hospital."

'I remember the little bonnets, they were so tiny and that stuck with me all my life. The lovely look on this old lady's face, and she said that she goes up to the hospital and gives them to the mothers so that they can bury their little babies in them. That would have been 35 years ago. I will never forget that.

'My mum lost my brother after me, it wasn't soon after birth, he had a hole in the heart and Down syndrome.

'It just wasn't talked about, and I remember Mum just always being really, really quiet and soldiering on. It wasn't until about ten years ago that Mum said it was such a terrible time, because Dad was so stoic and didn't want to know and there was the three of us kids. There was no support network at all for grief, losing babies.

'People just thought, *How terrible for you*, and never said anything about it. Mum said back then there was no one to talk to about losing a baby at all, and that's why to be able to offer those services in grief counselling like Bonnie

Babes, just talking about things, making it feel like you are not the only one in the world who's going through it and that it's all right.

'I remember that a friend of mine, I was having babies everywhere, and my friend was trying to have a baby and she couldn't fall pregnant. And then she did and then she lost the baby really early, but she had been trying so hard for so long. When she came over and I asked how she was.

'I could see the look on her face and we just hugged.

'When I was at primary school, it was 30 years ago, but I was amazed the teacher in our class one day said, "Hands up who's lost a brother or sister?" There were about five or six kids who put their hand up and I thought, *This is amazing*, even as a kid, to think that there are lots of families who like ours had lost a child. I was really shocked to see how many that had affected.

'My sister, her third boy was born – she had a terrible pregnancy and he was born with cerebral palsy. She was in hospital with him for so long, and the same thing, they don't know what to say, so they don't go. She was very alone.

'One of her friends had a very difficult birth, and the baby was not breathing for 20 minutes; when she heard about it she went straight up there because, she said to me, "If Annie is going through what I went through and is going to have a disabled child, then she needs all the help she can get."

'As a mother, everything that happens to the kids is [I feel] somehow my fault. So I can imagine what a mother thinks when she loses her baby, a lot of it would be, *What did I do wrong?*

'It is such a silent personal grief that even the husbands don't understand sometimes or can't relate to it, because pregnancy is just this primal thing and it affects every cell in your body. To lose a baby suddenly would be a nightmare.'

Rebecca Gibney's story
Rebecca Gibney is an actor who has won a number of awards, including the TV Week Gold Logie and Silver Logie for Most Popular Actress. She has a son, Zachary. Rebecca is also a Patron of the Bonnie Babes Foundation.

'I have been very fortunate in that when I decided I would try to get pregnant it happened very quickly and I had a "textbook pregnancy" where all things went okay, even though I was considered geriatric at 39.

'I have a friend who lost a baby in the final weeks of her pregnancy. It was devastating to her obviously and it had a profound effect on me as we worked together not long after she had gone through it. Her strength and honesty were incredible and her ability to deal with the tragic loss with such integrity and openness will stay with me forever.'

After witnessing her friend dealing with her loss and her subsequent support, Rebecca decided to become a Patron of the Bonnie Babes Foundation.

'I think it's imperative we support organisations like Bonnie Babes. I was approached by the Bonnie Babes Foundation after I had appeared in an episode of *GP* where I played a woman who gives birth to a stillborn baby. At that stage I had not given birth myself and the script had really touched me deeply so I was honoured to be asked to be a Patron. I often think that we take the miracle of childbirth for granted and being a mother myself I don't think there is anything more important.'

The figure of one in four pregnancies ending in a loss hasn't changed for many, many years. Rebecca still finds it hard to believe that this is a figure that is remaining steady within Australia, a first world country.

'I didn't know the figures before I joined the Bonnie Babes Foundation and I think it's staggering that we are still seeing the same problems occurring now. Having travelled to a number of third world countries for World Vision, I would expect those figures there but not here in Australia. I also have to say that having witnessed mothers losing their children in places like Africa, they feel the same pain that we do when we lose a child here so I think it is vital that we get behind organisations like Bonnie Babes so they can continue to support families as they deal with what can be the most difficult and often devastating times in their lives.'

Judith Krause's story
Judith Krause is currently a grief counsellor for the Bonnie Babes Foundation.

'My interest in the Bonnie Babes Foundation arose from my experience of multiple loss. It included several miscarriages, two complicated ectopic pregnancies and subsequent IVF treatments. Sadly, the Bonnie Babes Foundation was not in existence at that time and although I searched widely for a skilled person with whom I could share my anguish and profound sense of loss, I was left feeling devastatingly lonely. Everywhere I went there were pregnant women and perfectly formed babies in prams. Never before had it been so evident.

'Reproductive loss raises numerous emotions. Like many of you, I experienced sadness, anger, guilt, a sense of hopelessness, a sense of failure and an endless yearning, which lasted a surprising number of years. With relevant post-graduate qualifications and considerable experience, I felt my skills may help other Bonnie Babes Foundation families. It was on this basis that I undertook the Bonnie Babes Foundation grief training and became a volunteer counsellor. I now train others to do the same. I am frustrated when I hear well-meaning people say "time heals", because it doesn't. I believe time allows us to better deal with the situation and our emotions.

'It is essential to recognise the courage it takes to make that initial call for support. I distinctly recall circling the telephone for days before I found the strength to make that call to investigate the availability of services. Sometimes, with nothing tangible to grieve, other family members and friends may not fully appreciate the intensity of the family's grief. The overwhelming sense of loss, including dreams and expectations, can facilitate feelings of disbelief, vulnerability and powerlessness. Some may even feel alienated. With gender differences in the experience of grief, it is recognised that the mother often experiences a greater bond, but the partner's loss cannot be overlooked or considered in a lesser way. A mutual support system within their relationship may alleviate acute and intense stress.

'As a counsellor, sometimes I respond to a call and I am met with silence. Sometimes families' tears flow readily. On other occasions people question their emotionally charged responses and the unfairness of their situation. Maybe knowing that someone has experienced something similar is enough. Words are not always necessary initially. Families are encouraged, however, to regularly share their story with caring friends and family and to call the Bonnie Babes Foundation line or access their GP as frequently as required. Additionally, families are advised of other relevant and appropriate community services. Within the boundaries of the law, confidentiality is respected and each call taken is considered unique. No two situations are the same but the emotions experienced are universal. They are, however, not always simultaneously experienced.

'I feel enormously privileged that Bonnie Babes families so openly share their stories. It is my hope that they find comfort in the knowledge that they are not alone. Sadly, one in four pregnancies ends in a loss, meaning there are many more understanding souls surrounding us than we realise. For me, caring and supporting others in their bereavement brings unbelievable rewards.

'It is important to effectively assist families through their distress and to help them understand that their "normal" life has changed as they reflect on their loss and adapt to their new circumstances. Families are sensitively reminded that moving through their grief, or trying for another baby, does not mean forgetting or abandoning their loved one. I am always touched by the many beautiful and heartfelt ways families have chosen to remember and celebrate special days, anniversaries or the bonding of the short life of this much-loved lost baby.

'It is paramount to maintain non-judgmental respect for different cultural aspects, be present and empathetically listen as families reflect upon their emotions, hopes, dreams and unique circumstances.'

I Celebrate Your Life, My Baby

At the Bonnie Babes Foundation we know and love Judith Durham for her humanitarian work: as a dedicated, compassionate and caring patron of the Bonnie Babes Foundation for the past ten years, and also as national patron of the Motor Neurone Disease Association and patron of the Injured Nurses' Support Group.

But the international public knows and loves Judith, of course, for her chart-topping years with The Seekers, and her celebrated solo concerts and albums, which include many of her original inspirational compositions.

As our own highly esteemed Ambassador, Judith wrote a special song dedicated to the Bonnie Babes Foundation. The song is called 'I Celebrate Your Life, My Baby', with music composed by Judith herself. Judith co-wrote the lyrics with two other very inspirational people, Rachel Stanfield-Porter and Simon Barnett, and with the kind permission of Musicoast it is printed overleaf as a beautiful and emotional poem.

I Celebrate Your Life, My Baby

Music by Judith Durham © 1998 Musicoast
Words by Judith Durham, Rachel Stanfield-Porter, Simon Barnett © 1998
Musicoast/Bonnie Babes Foundation

Where do I start? How do I feel?
Sad and empty, cheated and lonely.
You were my life. You were my babe.
I was so excited, I longed for you only.
Did I do wrong? Why did I lose you?
You lived here inside me. Tears I still cry.
Friends couldn't know just how much I was grieving;
Just you and Mummy were saying goodbye.

I celebrate your life, my baby. Celebrate our time together
Precious gift, human soul. Here in my heart you'll be forever.
Celebrate your life, my babe . . . celebrate your life.

How am I now? I think of you often
And sense that somehow your spirit has grown.
Oh I'm learning to cope and I'm learning to live,
But without you somebody's missing at home.
Oh silent my tears. Silent your heartbeat.
Still I remember warmth deep inside.
Showing their kindness, friends so well-meaning
Just say to accept that you lived and you died.

And if somebody asks me do I know what love is,
I'll smile about you, and although we did part,
Now, and for always, you're my little angel,
Tucked in the corner of my aching heart.

I celebrate your life, my baby. Celebrate our time together
Precious gift, human soul. Here in my heart you'll be forever.
Celebrate your life, my babe . . . celebrate your life.

Acknowledgements

To the four most important reasons I started the Bonnie Babes Foundation and why I wrote *Small Miracles* – my beautiful boys. To Ezra and Joshua, I will always remember and celebrate the short time I had with you, and to Daniel and Joel, I am so proud of both of you, the caring, compassionate and loving young teenage boys you have become. I feel so blessed to have you both in my life.

To my closest friend Debbie Chalmers, the girl who almost finishes my sentences, for all the late-night cups of herbal tea to keep us going, the dedication and for the truly wonderful person you are, I thank you from the bottom of my heart.

Thanks to every family who participated in the book for your courage and strength in coming forward so that you could help others.

Thanks to Jacinta Di Mase from Jacinta Di Mase Management for making this happen and never giving up. For her tenacity and compassion for the Charity and volunteering her time selflessly. You have such an amazing strength of character.

My thanks to Helen Littleton and Louise Sherwin-Stark from Hachette Australia for believing in this book, for knowing right from the start just how much this publication is needed and how many people it will reach, and for being so amazing to work with. I would like to say a special thanks to Kate Ballard from Hachette Australia for being the driving force behind meeting our deadlines, her amazing dedication to the project and for knowing just the right thing to say when needed.

Thanks to our wonderful Queensland President, Barbara Short, who certainly ensures the Queensland branch of the Bonnie Babes Foundation works closely with the community and helps many families every year.

Thanks to the following hotels for their support with allowing families to tell their stories in a quiet way and to participate in interviews and for the donated accommodation provided: Rydges World Square, Sydney; The Como, Melbourne; Sheraton Mirage Resort and Spa, Gold Coast; Brisbane Marriot Hotel; Diamant Boutique Hotel, Canberra.

Finally, thanks to the following companies for assisting us with volunteers' travel: Premier Cabs, Sydney; 13CABS, Melbourne; Canberra Elite Taxis/Aerial Capital Group; Yellow Cabs (Qld) Pty Ltd.